I0819455

GOOD
LUCK

CASSANDRA EASON

NEW YORK

The reader is advised that this book is not intended to be a substitute for an assessment by, and advice from, an appropriate legal, financial, or mental health professional or other qualified expert.

ISBN 978-1-4549-6287-8
ISBN 978-1-4549-6288-5 (e-book)

Library of Congress Control Number: 2025022444

Union Square & Co. books may be purchased in bulk for business, educational, or promotional use. For more information, please contact your local bookseller or the Hachette Book Group's Special Markets department at special.markets@hbgusa.com.

Printed in China

10 9 8 7 6 5 4 3 2 1

unionsquareandco.com

Cover design by Nolan Pelletier
Interior design by Stacy Wakefield Forte
Image on page 53 by Shutterstock.com/Beskova Ekaterina

The book is dedicated to my children, Tom, Jade, Jack, Miranda, and Bill, and my grandchildren, Freya, Oliver, Holly, and Sophie, who daily remind me how lucky I am.

CONTENTS

Introduction

WELCOME TO LUCK

In the early 1960s, UK television astrologer Evadne Price signed off her daily show with the phrase "Think lucky and you'll be lucky!" In other words, the luckier we feel and act, the luckier we will become. More recently, "lucky girl syndrome" took the social media world by storm. In an article in *Harper's Bazaar*, author Mel Robbins explains the phenomenon: Essentially, if you tell the cosmos how fortunate you are, this good fortune will manifest and remain in your life. Good psychology, yes—but also perhaps evidence of something more, something hard to explain scientifically or even logically. Although for the most part we no longer believe, as did our distant ancestors, that bad luck is caused by evil spirits, we may be able to charge the energies around us to attract good luck and repel misfortune in ways we still do not fully understand.

This book suggests numerous ways to facilitate that charge, ensuring that luck-bringing processes animate your everyday life so good fortune fills your world.

LUCKY CHARMS AND RITUALS IN ACTION

Before a special occasion, many people often rely on charms and repetitive rituals to keep luck flowing. The early nineteenth-century composer Ludwig van Beethoven counted exactly sixty beans before grinding his coffee each morning, creating an auspicious environment for creativity—and he of course overcame deafness to create nine symphonies, thirty-two piano sonatas, and an opera, so ostensibly it worked. The golfer Tiger Woods wears a red shirt on the last day of tournaments, which is usually a Sunday, because Tiger was born on a Sunday and red is the lucky color for Sunday in Thailand, where his mother was born (for more on lucky colors, see pages 32–35). The Harry Potter series author J. K. Rowling types her title page only after the whole book is completed.

HOW DO WE ATTRACT LUCK?

With games of chance, successful gamblers develop an uncanny instinct for when a bet or roulette turn will be lucky and when to hold back. This finely tuned instinct is overwritten by those who gamble without discrimination time after time and are listening to wishful thinking, not intuition.

This book suggests tried-and-tested charms, as well as formulas and mini-rituals—like Beethoven's coffee-bean counting—that seem to kick-start and maintain the flow of luck. Luck is like a psychic snowball, growing bigger and bigger the more you reach out for it. This is confirmed by positive results after you combine a lucky charm, action, or words with an understanding of the difference between instinct and false optimism or doubt, which I discuss in this book.

BRINGING LUCK IN DREAMS

Dreams, too, can herald good fortune, whether you are visited by a grandmother who passed long ago now offering lucky lottery numbers or you experience foresight of a time and place where love or an opportunity awaits.

In the dream state, our unconscious mind overrides conscious thought so we are prompted to listen to and act upon signals around us that we may normally miss. Young children, whose minds are not cluttered with logic and deduction, have an knack for predicting lucky numbers. Whatever the source, a sudden foresight in dreams or a blinding flash of insight, if recognized, can open the way to what we call a "stroke of luck."

SELF-FULFILLING PROPHECY

Occasionally we may experience this insight in daily life. When you feel this sudden urgency, which can feel like the caffeine rush of very strong coffee, you should act on it immediately. This is the most important signal your body can give you and trumps any artificial method of improving your chances. Some gamblers use computers to narrow the odds of betting on horse or dog races, which is useful but rarely as spectacular as that flash of *now is the moment*.

This impulse is a self-fulfilling prophecy, and one that works both ways. When something goes wrong, we may blame it on bad luck, when in reality it may be the result of another's inefficiency or malice or our own oversight. In such cases, we may react to one bad occurrence by becoming overly anxious and cautious and hesitate more than we should—and then we make mistakes as a result of our panic, rendering us more likely to attract more what can be called "bad" luck. Conversely, perhaps we are given a new pendant and wear it on an occasion when we do not expect to succeed. Matters go brilliantly, so next time we put on the pendant before a significant occasion and we recall the previous good luck and unconsciously shine. If we can't find the pendant, we panic until it is restored.

By repeating actions and words each time you use a charm or carry out an action, you are tapping into energy sources humans do not fully understand but seem to work. Luck-wise, that is what matters. Think of Beethoven counting his coffee beans, triggering creativity and drawing him to people who could further his musical career and guiding them to him. How often have you met or been contacted by someone you were inexplicably thinking of, and usually they of you, although you may not have communicated for years—and they are just the person you need for help or information? Psychics call this telepathy, mind-to-mind communication, or simply an underused human ability employed when the smartphone runs out of battery. By following through on such seemingly chance encounters, you find an unmissable opportunity that even a day before or after would not have been available.

HOW TO MAKE YOUR OWN LUCK USING THIS BOOK

This book is filled with the makings of charms or ritual action that you can employ before an event where luck is needed. I encourage you to repeat this action regularly, because over time it will build up the energies of good fortune. By creating a routine, a talisman, or an object of focus, you can develop a repository of power that you can access at crucial times to release the energies of good luck and dull the doubt that may cause bad luck.

There are many suggestions in the pages ahead. Some are more contemporary, but many are based on folklore and tradition that date back to ancient times. A symbol from an old culture may carry the energies of all who have used it over hundreds or thousands of years. Read through these suggestions with an open mind to see if you are drawn to a charm or symbol, even if it is not one that you are familiar with or one that logically fits with the luck you'd like to attract.

There are many different good luck symbols represented in this book, including some from cultures that may be unfamiliar to you. Although many people find that they are drawn to symbols from their ancestors, the universal power of symbols from around the world can be accessed by anyone who treats them with respect. For example, countless households worldwide have Chinese frogs or toads with coins in their mouths, which are said to bring wealth and good fortune. The three-legged Chinese money toad, often made of jade or gold, is the power creature of Liu Hai, the god of prosperity, a Taoist deity that may predate the tenth century BCE. We can tap into the accumulated vibes of all those millennia to attract and generate wealth.

YOU CAN CHANGE YOUR LUCK

Maybe some spiteful relative told you about a family curse that means you are naturally unlucky. Logically you may know that such dire prophecies are never true, but when things go wrong for whatever reason, doubts can creep in. Or perhaps you are trapped in a loop of self-fulfilling prophecy and can't seem to break out of it. Whatever the reason, reversing imagined or coincidental bad luck is totally possible. This book devotes a chapter to this practice, so refer to chapter 7 if you feel beset by negative energies that you just can't shake.

HOW TO USE THIS BOOK

Beyond designating a charm or talisman to access whenever you need a bit of luck, you'll find that many of the lucky colors, numbers, jewelry, and age-old good luck rituals from around the world described in this book are most successful when applied to certain occasions. From choosing the luckiest date for a vacation or most auspicious wedding day to selecting the right house or location for a trip, you can keep this book on hand to help you in specific situations. By the end of the book, you will be adept at transferring good fortune to yourself and your life. Enjoy reading through these pages, and cheers to becoming the luckiest guy or girl in town!

LUCKY CHARMS
CHAPTER ONE

A lucky charm acts as a portable container for good luck that we carry with us. Keep these charms in your home or office, throw one in your bag, or even wear them as jewelry. You can collect charms over time and accumulate positive effects—I recommend you request them as presents because they are doubly lucky when gifted. In this chapter I describe lucky charms, lucky colors, statues, and symbols. As mentioned in the introduction, review them all with an open mind to see which resonate with you the most strongly!

Personal Signals

You may already have a personal indicator of approaching good fortune—for example, a distinctive bird that settled in the garden right before a happy event becomes for you an indicator that more blessings are on the way. Or perhaps you have a particular route that you prefer to walk to work or school before a major endeavor because it led you to success once. These signals may have risen out of serendipitous occurrences: For example, a familiar tune once heard in an unusual place becomes your music of choice before a personal trial. Maybe you saw a deceased relative's favorite flower blooming out of season, or a sequence of numbers whose appearance invariably proves lucky. These are powerful sources of good fortune, and the more you become aware of them, the more you can take advantage of the lucky vibes in the day ahead. How might this be possible? A personal signal puts you in a confident mood, so you radiate positivity to all you meet or contact, and in turn improve their mood so they are more helpful.

Natural Phenomena and Symbols

Here are just a few universal symbols of good luck.

ACORNS

This nut is lucky for bringing out untapped potential, especially if still in the cup. Use it to improve all long-term ventures, and one falling at your feet is most fortunate. An acorn is a reminder of the need for independence while valuing family roots, and it is lucky for family businesses. It is also associated with the Thanksgiving holiday.

CORNUCOPIA HORN OF PLENTY

A cornucopia is a curved hollow goat's horn, or more usually a horn-shaped basket containing fruit, vegetables, and grain. Kept in the kitchen, it should be used and the contents should be replaced regularly to keep abundance and goodwill flowing through the home. It is associated with feast-based holidays like Thanksgiving, when it may also contain nuts and fall leaves and often be used as a centerpiece, but its presence is equally applicable through the year as a luck-bringer.

FOUR-LEAF CLOVERS

One of the luckiest charms, the four leaves representing faith, hope, luck, and love.

HOLEY STONE

This is what it sounds like: a stone with a natural hole caused by water or weathering, found on riverbanks and seashore. A stone with three holes brings luck in the workplace, especially when hung on a knotted red cord tied with three knots. Suspended with dried yarrow over the marital bed, it promises lasting love. If you look through the hole of a natural stone at midnight during a full moon, you may see the future, fae, and benign ghosts, and most powerfully around Halloween.

ICE AND SNOW

Naturally melting ice or snow—or ice and snow placed in a pan over a weak light or on a stove to melt—dissipates anger, coldness, and estrangement in relationships, as well as general opposition and prejudice.

RAINBOWS

Rainbows are regarded as incredibly lucky in almost all cultures. Irish legend describes a crock of gold at the end of the rainbow that belongs to the fae, which can inspire the answer you have been seeking before the rainbow fades. Among the Indigenous people of New Zealand and parts of Australasia, a high-arched rainbow promises favor for any enterprise, and one forming a circle when seen in water or a double rainbow in the sky assures double success and happiness. In Western traditions, rainbows herald fulfillment of wishes, secret ambitions, and reconciliation.

When you see a rainbow, say aloud or in your mind the age-old rhyme "Rainbow, rainbow, magic measure, on the path I wend, let me find the treasure at the rainbow's end."

PRAYER STICK

For longer-term wishes, you'll want a prayer stick. To create one, first find a fallen branch (do not cut it from a tree). Strip the bark and place the branch in the ground. Thread wishes on luggage tags with organic red string or feathers into which you have spoken a wish, then tie them to the branch. Leave the wishes to blow away or decay in their own time. Alternatively, you can purchase Buddhist prayer streamers to hang outside, and when you touch each one, make a wish.

WISHBONE

Wishbone rings in silver or gold have a V-shaped point resembling an actual chicken or turkey wishbone. Customarily it is held by two people, then broken—the person with the biggest piece of the wishbone gets to make a wish. Wishbone rings are lucky for engagements and marriages or commitments, and the breaking of the actual wishbone is associated with feast-related holidays, including Thanksgiving, although it can occur whenever poultry is eaten.

Spiritually Significant Charms

The charms below have special spiritual power and are often associated with deeply held tradition or faith systems.

LAUGHING BUDDHA

This image is one of the most popular icons for bringing good fortune in every way. Some users do not specify a particular wish when they work with it, although others find the laughing Buddha effective as a focus for financial improvement. To employ the energy of the laughing Buddha:

- Set a small dish in front of a wooden or metal laughing Buddha and, if making an important petition, drape a circle of fresh flowers around the neck of the statue.
- Rub the tummy of the Buddha three times clockwise and ask no more than once a week for good fortune you need in any area of your life.
- If you need good news or recognition, name your desire and rub Buddha's right ear clockwise to receive results before the week is over.

KEYS

In ancient Greece, a key allowed wishes to reach the deities by unlocking the gate to the heavens. Other customs associated with keys include:

* Give a silver key charm to a young person on their eighteenth or twenty-first birthday to symbolically open opportunities.
* Silver keys are also powerful when worn by anyone seeking to open the door to a new job or career path or find the right home.
* Tie a key from a former home to a key from your new home and place them behind the front door to transfer the luck of a former dwelling to the new one.
* Follow the Japanese custom of giving to young people three key charms tied together or on a charm bracelet, signifying revealing the secrets of wisdom, love, and life.
* Silver or gold keys can be exchanged at a commitment ceremony to give your partner a lasting key to your heart, and are often found as ornaments at weddings.

FU XING, LU XING, AND SHOU XING

In the Chinese tradition, these are the three star gods of fortune, often seen in homes, restaurants, and financial institutions. They are customarily set in a row on a high shelf facing a dining table to bring abundance to the home. In a business, they are often found near where money or information is exchanged, whether face to face or via computer or phone.

Fu brings blessings, happiness, and good luck; Lu wealth, career success, and fertility; and Shou long life and health. Empower them by lighting incense sticks during the days of the Chinese New Year and every eighth day if they are working especially hard.

KWAN OR KUAN YIN

If you're looking for a boost in emotional or relationship good fortune, especially after loss or setback, a statue of the bodhisattva Kwan or Kuan Yin will be useful to you. A worldwide folk icon under different names throughout East and Southeast Asia, Kwan or Kuan Yin is the Tibetan Buddhist and Chinese goddess of compassion and good fortune.

BUDDHIST PRAYER WHEELS

For safe and happy car journeys or commuting, buy a solar-powered brass prayer wheel, place it on the dashboard, and ask for blessings on your journey.

Mythical Creatures

Creatures of myth and legend may not exist in the real world, but the awe they have inspired through generations creates a powerful good luck energy.

GARUDA

This deity is the protector of the good fortune of the home and is also fortuitous for travel and all matters of justice. Garuda is king of the birds in the Hindu religion and flies faster than the wind and even light, carrying Vishnu the preserver god on his back. Garuda has the head, red wings, talons, and beak of an eagle and the golden body and limbs of a man, with a pure white face.

PHOENIX

The phoenix is often pictured rising from its nest, heralding regeneration, long life, and revived health. Use it as a symbol of money returning, minor miracles occurring, and reviving ailing businesses. In the Western world, the glorious phoenix was a symbol of turning ordinary metals into gold. Ancient Greek legend says that it burns itself on a funeral pyre every five hundred years. From the ashes, as they turn golden, a new phoenix is born.

THUNDERBIRD

A First Nation symbol from North America and Canada, the thunderbird can be adopted respectfully as an image of power, fertility, potency, leadership, innovation, and accepting necessary change—even if not welcome. It also represents an awareness of the seasons and the evolving stages of life. The thunderbird is the bringer of rain, which pours from a lake on its back as it flies, while its flashing eyes create lightning and its vast eagle-like wings cause thunder. It crowns totem poles in North America and Canada. The thunderbird is often accompanied in flight by eagles or falcons.

Japanese legend also includes a thunderbird, which resembles a giant rook. It is a bird of the sun, creating thunder and lightning and guarding any approaches to the heavens.

UNICORN

The unicorn offers healing, loving communication, beauty, fertility, and a reminder that there is more to life than work and the material world. Viewing images of unicorns may have a calming effect and can be an enjoyable way to support focus and relaxation. As myth tells, the unicorn could run faster than light and walk across grass without disturbing it, and is fiercely protective of the innocent.

IRISH LEPRECHAUN

If placed in the garden, a ceramic leprechaun keeps good fortune flowing into your home and life, especially for speculation or gaming. A gold-colored coin should be buried on one side, a silver coin on the other, and a small ornamental hammer set horizontally in front of the statue for greater effect.

The leprechaun can be asked for luck, especially financial in nature, on Fridays. When a rainbow is in the sky or there's an urgent need for a lucky bet or other choice in speculation or gaming, hammer the ground in front of the leprechaun nine times while saying nine times, "Lucky Leprechaun, bring to me your crock of gold, that daily luckier I will be, with wealth untold."

GARDEN GNOME

The gnome is a more taciturn, slower-acting bringer of good luck, health, and prosperity to your home and all within it. Set a gnome statue made of colorful, brown, or gray pottery in your garden or among plants growing in a large pot.

Some households have a family of gnomes for ongoing luck. Each day, add a copper coin or disk to a dish in front of the largest gnome. As you drop it into the dish, say, "It is not your treasure I wish to possess, but continuing good fortune and success." When the dish is full, leave one coin in the dish and use the rest of the money to buy a plant to keep the luck growing.

DRAGONS

A gold-and-red dragon statue inside the front door protects the home and, in both Eastern and Western traditions, guards finances. The green dragon, one of the four celestial animals in feng shui, calls good health, fertility, and fresh energies into the home or workplace when placed on the east side of the home.

WISH BOXES OR PRAYER POTS

To focus a wish after it is written, as well as to preserve it, make a wish box or prayer pot. Find a container with a lid or slit to deposit, or post, your wishes. That could be a metal jar with a deity head as the lid, or perhaps a wooden box with a hinged lid, often with a painted image on it. Some people set the box near a source of warmth to symbolically incubate the wishes within it.

Externalizing wishes by writing and storing them increases energy within yourself, which can be directed toward the purpose of the wish. The first of the month and New Year's Day are customary days for wish box posting.

* Write one wish only, in as few words as possible; make sure you immediately act on it in the real world after posting.
* Build in a realistic time frame for fulfillment.
* Write your wish, fold the paper, and put it in the box; reciting the wish three times in rapid succession, whether out loud or in your mind.
* Only use this method once a month, and according to the cosmic balance sheet, do something positive in return.
* When the wish box is full, take out the pile of wishes, tie them with red cord in three knots, and burn them in a bonfire or a fire bucket with sand in the bottom.
* Bury the ashes under a fruit tree.

Lucky Metals

Metals bring the luck of the earth and thus symbolize material resources, especially as coins.

CHARM BRACELETS

A charm bracelet with various charms in gold or silver attracts different kinds of luck specific to the charms: a book for learning, a key or padlock for a new home or unlocking opportunity, a plane or boat for distant travel, and a heart locket for love.

COINS IN WATER

Casting coins in water has been considered a lucky practice for generations. For example, legend says that throwing groups of three coins into the eighteenth-century Trevi Fountain in Rome will grant wishes. Specifically, one coin guarantees you will return to Rome, two foretells that you will meet an Italian lover, and three means that you will marry them.

Around the world, coins are thrown into wishing wells for many kinds of wishes and the money is donated to charity as part of the cosmic exchange. Some existing wells were dedicated to St. Bridget or Brighid or the Mother Goddess, and are now called bridewells or ladywells. These are still considered potent places to wish for fertility.

COINS

Coins, especially older ones with precious metal content higher than it is today, are considered lucky. Give a coin in a new purse or wallet to avoid money draining from the recipient. Luckiest of all is any coin minted in your birth year, especially one no longer in circulation. Here are a few specific coins that can bring luck:

* In the United States, Mercury dimes—first issued in 1916 and continuing until 1945—are still considered to be luck-bringing. The image of Lady Liberty with the winged cap became rapidly associated with Mercury, the god of the crossroads and good fortune, who likewise wore a winged cap. Those minted in leap years are especially fortunate.

* Antique silver sixpences are much coveted in the United Kingdom; also lucky is the bronze Irish penny minted from 1928 to 1968, with the Irish harp on one side and a hen and chicks on the other.

* Chinese divinatory coins, especially three tied together with red string, are great for luck and prosperity in every way. Luckiest of all are groups of eight coins, and ten have a similar effect when used for health, fame, and success. Set them where money enters rather than is kept.

GOLD

Gold is the metal of the sun and is aligned with success, wealth, achieving ambitions, and finding lasting love. Re-empower gold jewelry by leaving it outside from dawn or the previous evening sunset until noon on the summer solstice, or longest day of the year, which falls in June.

HORSESHOE

Horseshoes are associated with St. Dunstan, the tenth-century blacksmith saint who in myth nailed the cloven-hoofed devil to his forge wall and said that henceforward none may enter where the horseshoe guarded the door. Traditionally a horseshoe is first placed outside of the front door of your home on the first of the month or on May 19, which is St. Dunstan's Day. On this day it is empowered by lighting a red candle. The horseshoe has become a symbol of domestic good fortune.

A silver horseshoe is carried by a newlywed couple to protect their happy home. Anyone can benefit from a full-sized iron horseshoe set over the front door outside the house, or inside the house over a fireplace. It should either point up to keep the luck in or point down to draw luck from the earth. Iron is the metal of Mars, originally thought to keep away the fae; use seven iron nails to attach your horseshoe to the doorframe or wall.

Dolls and Toys

Not just for the amusement of children, some beloved toys and figurines can be powerful containers of good fortune.

NENETTE AND RINTINTIN DOLLS

These woolen yarn dolls were originally produced during World War I in France and were meant to protect soldiers in the trenches, airmen, and their sweethearts and children back home. They were so popular that they spread to other countries, such as the Netherlands, Switzerland, and the United States. The mascot dolls must be given, not bought, and not one without the other—they are often joined by a single cord. Although they are rare now, they are especially worth seeking out if you wish to protect lovers far away.

WORRY DOLLS

Also known as trouble dolls, these small, handmade, fabric embroidered dolls in Mayan dress are originally from the Indigenous people of the Guatemalan highlands. They are created for children and adults to offload their worries and misfortunes. It is believed that putting the doll under your pillow helps to take all sorrows away during the night. Worry dolls can be purchased in family sets.

Lucky Colors

We all have preferred lucky colors that seem to make our life go right whenever we wear them. In the introduction, I described how golfer Tiger Woods favors red, following the traditions of his mother's homeland of Thailand.

LUCKY COLORS IN THE EAST

Thailand has a comprehensive lucky color system rooted in Hinduism, Buddhism, and astrology, which is echoed in other East and Southeast Asian countries, where each color is considered lucky on its own day of the week. By association, the color is therefore lucky for those born on that day. Certain colors are also fortunate for weddings, first dates, job interviews, auditions, and approaching a would-be lover.

Sunday: red is considered a lucky color in China and the rest of East and Southeast Asia; red envelopes of money are given on Chinese New Year and at weddings

Monday: yellow or cream

Tuesday: pink

Wednesday: green during the day, gray at night

Thursday: orange or brown

Friday: light blue

Saturday: purple

LUCKY COLORS IN THE WEST

Lucky colors that overlap in the most common Western and Eastern systems can amplify their effects.

Here are some common associations between colors and their properties in the West:

White: potential, energy, originality and innovations, bringing or restoring prosperity when fortunes are low, breaking a run of bad luck, all matters concerning fathers, good health; softer white for pregnancy, babies and children, mothers

Red: action, courage, positive sudden change, strength, determination, power, stamina, sexual passion, potency, competitiveness, resisting injustice, overcoming seemingly impossible odds

Orange: confidence, joy, all creative and artistic ventures, independence, self-esteem, strengthening identity, media success, music, fertility, strongly felt desires, overcoming food issues and cravings

Yellow: logic, learning, financial acumen, especially in speculation, technological expertise, memory, concentration, examinations and tests, all swift-moving matters, persuasion, adaptability, short-duration breaks, recovery through conventional healing

Green: love, fidelity, commitment, bringing beauty into your life, acquisition of beautiful possessions, harmony, the environment, for healing people through natural methods, the gradual increase of health, wealth, and material resources; along with red, said to be the luckiest of colors

Blue: idealism, acquired or traditional knowledge, leadership, justice through official means, career and employment (especially promotion), authority, long-distance or long-term travel and house moves, marriage and partnerships of all kinds, expansion of business

Purple: imaginative ventures, calling for messages in dreams (especially where deceased relatives bring information related to luck), finding answers through dreams, intuitive insights, discovering truth, contacting friends and family members with whom you have lost touch

Pink: peacemaking, reconciliation, happy family relationships, friendship, young or new love, growth of love and trust after betrayal

Brown: stability, security, reliability, resolving practical tasks or problems, animals, gradual accumulation of money, property, dealing with officialdom (such as banking), conservation of old places, finding what is lost or stolen

Gray: compromise, keeping a low profile, neutralizing unfriendly energies and feelings, negotiations, solving mysteries

Gold: high achievement, global matters, fulfilling a great dream or ambition, urgent or large infusion of money and resources, a long and happy life, a major leap forward, recognition and fame, recovering after a huge setback

All colors vibrate at different frequencies and affect us physically as well as psychologically and are an instant way of supercharging luck. Get colorful and you'll feel an instant difference!

Consider the following ways of integrating lucky colors into your life:

- Burn colors as candles.
- Buy flowers, especially fragrant ones so you inhale the color energy.
- Absorb as colored drinks or food.
- Wear clothing in that color, or have a collection of pillows or blankets according to the kind of luck you are seeking to attract.

SPECIAL OCCASIONS
CHAPTER TWO

Everything carries special luck-bringing qualities according to the number associated with it, which can be used to determine if it's right for a particular occasion or purpose. From choosing a new home or an auspicious date for a major event to deciding on the right name for a new business, baby, or pet, there are time-tested numerological systems to help you make the best choice. In this chapter I'll show you how, as well as how to match lucky numbers with your own personal or destiny number to supercharge your luck.

Calculating Lucky Numbers

Every letter has a numerical value. For example, A = 1, B = 2, and C = 3. Then double digits are added together; M = 13 is reduced to 4 when 1 + 3 is added together, P = 16 is reduced to 7 when 6 + 1 is added together, and so on, all the way to Z, the twenty-sixth letter of the alphabet, which reduces to 8 when 2 + 6 is added together. Add the total number values of the letters in the name of a venue, or when calculating the right home, vacation destination, or event, plus any relevant dates under question. The number values are then combined and reduced to a single digit (1 through 9), except for the two master numbers, 11 and 22, which are particularly fortunate.

All you need are the choice of dates, properties, locations, etc. and a calculator (unless you are good at mental math).

Hint: If you don't receive the numerical result you were hoping for, try changing the date or time of the actual event, or its spelling, to get a better result.

About the Numbers

The Pythagorean or ancient Greek system, based on the nine primary numbers—plus the master numbers of 11 and 22—is most commonly used in basic numerology.

The below chart is used for calculating important numerological numbers, such as your destiny number.

THE PYTHAGOREAN LETTER-TO-NUMBER

Correspondence Chart

1	2	3	4	5	6	7	8	9
A	B	C	D	E	F	G	H	I
J	K	L	M	N	O	P	Q	R
S	T	U	V	W	X	Y	Z	

THE NUMBER OF INNOVATION AND LEADERSHIP

Lucky qualities: independence, individuality, drive, assertiveness, strength, boundless energy; 1 is the initiator of action and the pioneer

- *For property:* brings luck in aiming high, whether a house that requires going above budget or that will, you believe, increase dramatically in value
- *For dates of events:* totally memorable, based entirely on the instructions of or organized by the person/couple/company whose milestone is celebrated
- *For a child/pet name:* as a babe does not like people fussing or cooing and from an early age will be ambitious and independent, a leader rather than a follower; the most prominent and characterful of a litter of animals
- *For a business name:* a trendsetter and a new slant on old ideas; successful self-employment
- *For travel:* solo adventures, singles' vacations, or runaway weddings/honeymoons

THE NUMBER OF NEGOTIATION AND PEACEMAKING

Lucky qualities: cooperation, adaptability, mediation, partnerships of all kinds, ability to see both sides of any question and weld disparate elements

- *For property:* a home that promises harmony within and with neighbors and community; intergenerational
- *For dates and events:* a happy, harmonious event with no quarrels or rivalries
- *For a child/pet name:* good-natured from their first day; later, a natural team player who will fit in with siblings/other pets
- *For a business name:* creates a feel-good factor and positive employer/employee and customer relations, favors partnerships
- *For travel:* uneventful and restful; for couples returning to a favorite location or a second honeymoon

THE NUMBER OF CREATIVITY AND THE SEEKER OF TRUTH

Lucky qualities: communication, written and verbal; charisma, persuasiveness, sociability, and creativity (especially in arts and entertainment); expansion of possibility; fertility in every way; generosity; a sense of justice

- *For property:* a home ideal for extensions and major improvements; no hidden snags
- *For dates and events:* good for anything meticulously planned and rehearsed, especially a show with singing and dancing
- *For a child/pet name:* a natural charmer and very sociable
- *For a business name:* good for networking/expansion, media connections
- *For travel:* beneficial for family or group vacations and touring

THE NUMBER OF REALISM AND CAUTION

Lucky qualities: stability and common sense, a practical foundation for ideas, skilled planning, loyalty, trustworthiness, organizational skills, and the ability to work within constraints; a firm grasp of reality

- *For property:* a safe investment, and good for longer-term/forever moves; good for long-lease renters
- *For dates and events:* a sign that the event will proceed as planned, with no good or bad surprises; for formal celebrations and anything associated with older people
- *For a child/pet name:* reliable, although if given to a newborn, may indicate a child who may come to be timid in unfamiliar settings; good for pets who will be alone during the day
- *For a business name:* a secure investment with moderate success but longer-term stability
- *For travel:* delivers what was promised online or in the brochure and is likely a value for the money; indicates a familiar haunt that will bring happiness

THE NUMBER OF VOYAGING AND THE ENTREPRENEUR

Lucky qualities: love of adventure and eagerness for new knowledge and experiences, especially distant places; a willingness to take a chance on future success; luck in speculation; quick to learn, but perhaps easily distracted

- *For property:* indicates that the right home may appear suddenly, but could involve a change of location and lifestyle or have unusual features; auspicious for short-term renters
- *For dates and events:* good for a fun and informal event, which may involve games; especially lucky if children are involved
- *For a child/pet name:* has curious, restless, and unpredictable energy; this name is often assigned to those who are unusually alert; if a pet, could be a natural escapee
- *For a business name:* fortuitous for home-based businesses; strong for those who rely on online networking or frequent work-based travel
- *For travel:* last-minute vacations to unfamiliar destinations and any vacation that may be on the short side; could hint at a trip that is a combination of work and leisure

THE NUMBER OF LOVE AND PROTECTION OF THE WEAK

Lucky qualities: altruism, protection of the vulnerable, nurturing toward both close loved ones and the world in general, sympathy, idealism, compassion, tolerance of others' weaknesses, romance and lasting commitment

- *For property:* could make a great love nest, secret or otherwise; indicates harmony in a shared accommodation; a home for a couple wanting a family or a settled lifestyle
- *For dates and events:* a successful event for friends and family, bringing reconciliation of differences and estrangements
- *For a child/pet name:* an affectionate child or pet who needs extra tactile care and hates being alone; from a young age, a child with this name will naturally care for those in need. If it's a pet, they'll have a nurturing instinct, especially toward younger animals.
- *For a business name:* lucky for any business where customer care and ethics are central; possibly part of a collective or franchise
- *For travel:* good for meeting new people and organized holidays where comfort supersedes luxury; not for seekers of solitude

THE NUMBER OF WISDOM, SELF-CONTAINMENT, AND SPIRITUALITY

Lucky qualities: spiritual powers, the ability to see what is coming over the horizon, introspection, secrecy, powers of healing (both conventional and alternative), love of beauty and harmony, ability to move to the next stage and with the cycles of life, often a Heart number (also known as your heart's true desire number), as is 6

- *For property:* a home, getaway vehicle, or chalet somewhere remote and beautiful
- *For dates and events:* for outdoor events such as a handfasting, beach, or forest wedding
- *For a child/pet name:* good for a child or pet who sometimes seems otherworldly, sensitive, and wise beyond years; people will say that anyone with this name has "been here before"; some believe a deceased pet can come back in this form and find you
- *As a business name:* for creating beauty or offering a therapy such as psychotherapy, physiotherapy, or spiritual teaching
- *For travel:* a vacation for solitary pursuits or withdrawal from the world to the wilderness, maybe with a loved one; could be a spiritual retreat or seminar

THE NUMBER OF POWER AND PROSPERITY

Lucky qualities: status-oriented, power-seeking, filled with confidence, focused aims, and energy, as well as acumen for business and finance, efficiency, and proficiency in any chosen field; logic

- *For property:* a home with the latest modern conveniences, or a possible renovation in an up-and-coming neighborhood
- *For dates and events:* good for a big formal event with many guests with no expense spared
- *For a child/pet name:* demands constant attention but is incredibly rewarding; for a pet who won't like getting muddy but will do well being shown
- *For a business name:* for a business that will make significant money and gain prestige, especially for luxury goods
- *For travel:* truly five-star experience; could indicate an all-inclusive resort

THE NUMBER OF ACTION AND THE CRUSADER

Lucky qualities: courage, desire for perfection, humanitarianism, impulsiveness, intolerance for prejudice or inaction, honesty without tact, a refusal to be deterred no matter the obstacle

- *For property:* the right home that will tick every box; for those who need plenty of space inside and outside
- *For dates and events:* hints at a celebration that is action-packed from beginning to end with lots of guest participation; unusual venues
- *For a child/pet name:* a good name for a baby who can never sit still and will grow into a child with innumerable activities; for a pet, one who will be happiest off the leash; a tiny pet with the heart of a lion(ess)
- *For a business name:* for an enterprise that will rapidly become a market leader, perhaps involving risks (although ones that usually pay off)
- *For travel:* may involve extreme sports or exploring places off the beaten track

THE NUMBER OF INTUITION AND THE DREAMER

Lucky qualities: instincts, ingenuity, psychic awareness, a dreamer whose nighttime and daytime vision may prove groundbreaking, insight into the unspoken motives and intentions of others

- *For property:* may indicate a new place set back from the road, shrouded by trees or bushes, or, if communal, the entrance and windows may be covered with plants and elaborate blinds; this home has room for a personal sanctuary
- *For dates and events:* a themed or romantic event
- *For a child/pet name:* a babe often lost in dreams and with a love of color and music from their first day; for a pet, this will be good for an animal who has acute senses and is an ideal helper for humans
- *For a business name:* for handcrafted or designed goods or customized services
- *For travel:* a previously unvisited location or an unusual destination for a vacation

THE NUMBER OF THE EAGLE AND THE MASTER BUILDER

Lucky qualities: a shaper of policy, global thinking; nobility of thought and action; joining of reason and intuition, logic, and feeling; vision and practicality; energy and compassion

- *For property:* a home that may stretch resources to buy and requires much DIY work but is ultimately a future palace
- *For dates and events:* good for an exotic or tropical overseas gathering, perhaps a wedding with a small group of guests
- *For a child/pet name:* the right name for someone alert and attentive from day one, who is developmentally advanced; for a pet, one who stands out from the pack and seems much older or more aware than others
- *For a business name:* good for a one-person operation, or for a recently acquired run-down business that will be turned around and flourishing a relatively short time after acquisition
- *For travel:* good for an influencer trip or for those writing a book or hoping to record a podcast; an excellent opportunity for a potential travel writer

Personal Destiny Energy

You can supercharge that luck even further by combining the number of an event with your own personal energies as expressed in your destiny number (determined by your full name at birth, representing your life's purpose and path), and your personal birth number (derived from your birth date, reflecting your challenges and innate tendencies).

FINDING YOUR DESTINY NUMBER

Your destiny number is the go-to number against which you can match any other using the formulas described in this chapter. If the date for the chosen event or the number corresponding to your preferred house or business name matches your destiny number, that extra alignment means that you're in for an additional boost of luck. The destiny number is found by adding the numbers of your full name together and reducing to a single digit (or the master numbers 11 or 22). Simply add the separate digits of your name:

First name LEZA: L = 3, E = 5, Z = 8, A = 1 → 3 + 5 + 8 + 1 = 17 → 1 + 7 = 8
Middle name JANE: J = 1, A = 1, N = 5, E = 5 → 1 + 1 + 5 + 5 = 12 → 1 + 2 = 3
Last name BRANDEN: B = 2, R = 9, A = 1, N = 5, D = 4, E = 5, N = 5 → 2 + 9 + 1 + 5 + 4 + 5 + 5 = 31 → 3 + 1 = 4
Add together the reduced numbers: 8 + 3 + 4 = 15 → 1 + 5 = 6
Final Destiny Number: 6

In some cases, you may need to make multiple separate calculations to match your destiny numbers with individual aspects. For example, if you're seeking both the most fortuitous venue for an event as well as your vacation destination and date, you may wish to calculate each separately.

Finding the Best Date for an Event

First choose a proper noun representing the event, its location, the venue, or whatever feature of the occasion you desire to determine luck for. Then add the numbers of the complete date on which it will occur. Numerically reduce these larger numbers and try to align with your destiny number if you want the perfect match. If two people are choosing a wedding date or venue, they should add their destiny numbers together. In the same way, if a fortuitous date for your parents' anniversary party is desired, use their combined destiny numbers. For a company event, compare the reduced number representing the name of the company to a number representing the purpose of the event combined with the number for the chosen date or venue.

Choosing the Luckiest House

If you are house hunting, you can use this technique to make a decision between various prospective homes. First, narrow down your choice to three or four potential dwellings that fit your financial and practical criteria.

HEAD OR HEART ALIGNMENT?

In some cases, a desire may be close to your heart but opposes the numbers you are calculating. This does not make your calculations wrong, but it does throw an emotional wrench into the works. For example, your parents are planning a big white wedding for you and your beloved in a cathedral with eight bridesmaids and ten groomsmen in satin shorts, but what you really want is an informal woodland wedding for only immediate family. Your destiny number may not match what is on offer.

See what is going on numerically and emotionally behind the scenes. Perhaps your *parents'* destiny number, or even the destiny number from one parent, may be aligning with those elaborate wedding plans. In that case, you may have to decide: head or heart? Once you do make up your mind and choose whether going along with the royal-style soiree your mother has planned and saved for since you were in the cradle or pursuing your own desires, you can embrace the luck attached to that choice because the decision was made with love.

As you calculate the numerical value of each, use the *precise* address as written on the real estate details or online advertisement. Keep address numbers as numbers, and, if overseas, include the country.

Add any house name and its number, plus the street or lot name, district/town/city/county/state, and country, reducing each letter in the address to numbers. Once you have those numbers, reduce to a single digit, or 11 or 22. If you want to be super accurate about your luck, check if your single destiny number (or, if part of a pair, your destiny numbers added together) is aligned with your numerical choice of property.

The Luckiest Baby Name

Read through the meanings of each number listed earlier in this chapter, taking note of the characteristics that they embody.

To choose an appropriate first name for a newborn baby, calculate the numbers of the names you are considering to see which reflects the characteristics the baby is already manifesting. The personality of a baby can be felt in the womb and in the early days after birth as the infant stamps their identity onto the world. The early days of a newborn's life are filled with clues—for example, a baby who from the first day is looking around, never sleeps, and constantly reaches out would be a curious, mercurial 5 and therefore need a corresponding name. You can also build into this first name the aspirations and qualities you would like your child to develop.

If there is no numerical alignment with a preferred name, try altering the spelling slightly—for example, try Tom instead of Thomas. If this still does not feel right, ask if it is the grandparents' choice or family tradition, and not yours, that is influencing a new babe's name. Go for the name you feel best reflects the infant's unmistakable character and the qualities you desire for them. Focus on first and middle names, not surnames.

In some Indigenous societies, such as the Squamish and Lil'wat nations of British Columbia, Canada, a child's true name is not given until their teenage years or even later. Until then, they may have a different first or middle name with a different numerical value, allowing for personal growth and evolving personality traits. This practice acknowledges that a child's identity develops over time and provides the opportunity to choose a name that aligns more accurately with their true self.

Pet Names

Much like newborn children, pets also reveal distinct characteristics when you first meet them, whether you pick them out of a litter or first get to know them at a rescue center, and that will influence their future name. You can align the numerical value of a chosen name with the destiny number calculated from their birth or adoption date.

DAYS & DATES

★ CHAPTER THREE ★

There is still more nuance to be found in the innate luckiness of each day, month, year, and even hour, both in its own right and for different needs. In this chapter, you can mix and match wisdom about the good fortune accompanying different dates and times to obtain the maximum luck for anything. Whether applying for a loan, bidding on an item online, seeking a new job, entering a competition, or investing money, there is always a right time and place. Bonus: you won't need to do any calculations!

Lucky Months

Of all features of a date, the month may contain the strongest luck factor and is not reliant on number values. Each month has luck specific to certain endeavors, or times when good fortune flows so much more easily. If you combine this with the right day of the week and the correct date number and year (if relevant), the balance will tip even further in your favor. You can use the lucky flowers and crystals of the month listed here as good luck talismans to supercharge your luck even more.

AUGUST

August is considered the luckiest month overall. It was named after the Roman emperor Augustus Caesar because several major lucky events in his life happened during that month.

August is a fortunate month for reversing bad luck or loss, for gaining opportunities previously denied, and for opening doors that have been closed.

Flowers: gladiolus, marguerite daisy

Crystals: jade, peridot, moss agate, opal

SEPTEMBER

September is named after *septem*, the Latin word for "seven," because it was the seventh month after the New Year on the oldest known Roman calendar, which had only ten months in a year.

This month is lucky for gaining knowledge, finding justice, and using persuasion to obtain desired results. September is the best month for signing contracts, finding solutions for difficult questions, and resolving long-standing relationship difficulties.

Flowers: aster (known best as the purple, pink, or white starlike autumnal Michaelmas daisy), blue lobelia

Crystals: blue sapphire, as gem or unpolished, traditionally worn when treaties were signed; blue topaz, aquamarine

OCTOBER

October's name comes from the Latin word *octo* because it was the eighth month in the old Roman calendar after the New Year. October is lucky for financial advantage, major moneymaking, property acquisition, profitable results from an earlier investment, and starting over in a new place or career.

Flowers: mimosa, marigold

Crystals: obsidian, black pearl, blue aqua and aura quartz, quartz bonded with gold

NOVEMBER

November's name comes from the Latin word *novem*, which means "nine," because it was the ninth month in the old Roman calendar. November represents luck in aiming high, replacing the old and redundant with the new and potentially promising, and manifesting dreams and desires.

Flowers: chrysanthemum, red poppy of remembrance

Crystals: yellow topaz, ruby, turquoise

DECEMBER

Named after the Latin word *decem*, meaning "ten," December is the tenth month after the New Year in the old Roman calendar. December is also representative of ten as the number of unity, so it is an excellent time for celebrations with family and friends and represents the return of optimism and enthusiasm.

Flowers: poinsettia, Christmas cactus

Crystals: amazonite, malachite, opal aura quartz, snowflake obsidian

JANUARY

January is ruled by Janus, the Roman god of gates and doorways, who has two faces looking in opposite directions. This month is lucky for speedy resolution of what was not completed in December, for new beginnings in every way, for successfully quitting bad habits, and for discovering new friends.

Flowers: snowdrop, crocus

Crystals: snow quartz, white howlite, garnet

FEBRUARY

Named after the Roman festival of fertility and purification held on February 15, the festival of Februa became combined with the love and fertility festival

Lupercalia held on the same day, from which we get St. Valentine's Day.

February is lucky for awakening new love and trust, increasing good fortune in every way, and for melting coldness or indifference.

Flowers: daffodil, wisteria

Crystals: amethyst, coral, bloodstone, all fluorites

MARCH

Watch out for an especially lucky March when it falls in a leap year. On March 1, be the first in your family or friends to say "white rabbits" to herald the new month and bring you good luck throughout the month.

Named after Mars, the Roman god of war and agriculture, March increases good fortune if exploring new territory and adventures. It is also good for the restoration of physical strength, tackling bullies or inequality wherever it may be found, and finding independence from the approval of others.

Flowers: geranium, hibiscus, hollyhock

Crystals: orange carnelian, diamond, Herkimer diamond, bloodstone

APRIL

April is named after Aphrodite, Greek goddess of love, the sea, and beauty, and after Aprilis, goddess of the Etruscans, the people who once inhabited central Italy. April brings luck in domestic matters, love, and fertility, as well as creativity and acquiring valuable artifacts or possessions.

Flowers: bluebell, rose, tulip

Crystals: jade, green chrysoprase, rose quartz

MAY

May is named after Maia, the Roman maiden goddess of spring and warmth. May is a lucky time for adoption, for fostering and good relations with stepchildren, for women seeking to conceive by artificial insemination, for single mothers and fathers, as well as for couples using in vitro fertilization.

Flowers: lavender, lilac, lily of the valley

Crystals: citrine, flower jasper, white sapphire

JUNE

June is named after Juno, Roman goddess of marriage, who is the protectress of women and rules over the fruitful harvest to come. This month is the most fortunate of all for marriage and love commitment, fidelity, partnerships of all kinds, and fertility.

Flowers: lily, hydrangea, red rose

Crystals: emerald, imperial jade, green garnet

JULY

Formerly called Quintilis, the fifth month in the early Roman calendar, July received its name from the Roman emperor Julius Caesar, who believed himself an earthly representative of the god Jupiter.

July is lucky for attaining power and high ambitions, leadership, potency, and acquiring traditional knowledge, as well as for justice and exotic or long-distance vacations.

Flowers: larkspur (a form of delphinium), passionflower, sunflower

Crystals: clear crystal quartz, golden topaz, yellow spinel

Lucky Days of the Week

Each day of the week has its own luck-bringing powers—even Friday, despite old superstition giving it a bad reputation, linking it with the Crucifixion and the day of the week when the fae ruled with trickery. You can also *make* each day of the week especially lucky for you by wearing its associated colors, lighting colored candles, or buying colored flowers related to a particular day (see also pages 32–35 for more information on lucky colors).

SUNDAY

Sunday is lucky for personal fulfillment and achieving ambitions, power, and success, as well as all matters concerning fathers and mature men; for new beginnings, prosperity, and self-confidence.

Color: gold

MONDAY

This day is good for luck in domestic and family matters, and for women—especially mothers and grandmothers—and children. It is lucky for fertility (along with Friday) and for protection, especially while traveling overseas.

Color: silver

TUESDAY

Tuesday is ideal for any situation in which you must take initiative. It is a day for independence, resisting injustice, overcoming seemingly impossible odds, passion, the consummation of love, physical strength, and young men and women in the armed forces or services.

Color: red

WEDNESDAY

Wednesday is best for luck in moneymaking ventures, clear communication, persuasion, adaptability, and versatility, as well as for mastering new technology and for short-distance travel, house moves, renting, and weekend vacations.

Color: yellow

THURSDAY

For all-around good luck, Thursday is the most fortuitous. It is also the day most aligned with career, especially self-employment and success; long-distance travel and house moves; justice through courts or official channels; marriage and permanent relationships from midlife onward; fidelity (for which Friday is also lucky); potency; and for banishing excesses and addictions.

Colors: blue, purple

FRIDAY

For luck in attracting love, especially for young men and women, Friday is the day. It is also the day of arts and crafts, friendships, mending quarrels, fertility, and all women's health matters. Friday is the luckiest day for reducing the influence of destructive lovers and possessiveness.

Colors: green, pink

SATURDAY

For good luck regarding unfinished business, slow-moving matters, property acquisition, and profitable sales, Saturday is the luckiest day. It is also a good day to establish boundaries around yourself and your property, and for banishing debt.

Colors: brown, gray, indigo, dark purple

Lucky Days of the Month

An alternative to using the day names Monday, Tuesday, etc. or reducing the date numbers to single digits, this method uses the full date number, such as 21 (not reduced to 3), for extra information. See which method you prefer. Different date meanings can be useful for fine-tuning. The number 1 refers to the first of the month, 2 to the second, and so on. The first nine echo the 1 through 9 meanings, as explained in the previous chapter, and the 11 and 22 in this chart augur particularly well.

1 New beginnings

2 Balance and negotiation

3 Expansion

4 Caution

5 Clear communication

6 Peace

7 The unknown

8 Taking the power

9 Calculated risks worth taking

10 Unity and agreements

11 Following instincts

12 Justice

13 Property (despite superstitions, this is not an unlucky number)

14 Innovation

15 Rebuilding links

16 Health

17 Securing contracts and agreements

18 Resolution leading to victory

19 Strength through independence

20 Partnerships

21 Gaining status and authority (helpful in power struggles)

22 Limitless potential

23 Success in exams and tests, and dividends through speculation

24 Fidelity and loyalty

25 Restoring what or whom is lost or estranged

26 Transforming a situation through words

27 Travel, initiating action, owed money returned

28 Creative success and fame

29 Finding the truth or sharing a secret

30 Celebrations and financial advantages

31 Family, home, stability

Lucky Years

Different years emphasize different forms of luck, and year dates may be relevant when seeking ideal time frames or anticipating results. If, for example, you are planning a course that will take three years, evaluating the date three years into the future may give you guidelines for how to bring luck in to improve outcomes.

LET'S TRY A FEW:

2026 and **2035** are both **1** years, favoring new beginnings, results within the year, independence, fame and fortune, leadership, wealth, health, and happiness, as well as all matters involving fathers.

2027 and **2036** are both **2** years, when harmony, partnerships, twin souls, and negotiations are favored. It's the right time to launch a second career, and it helps those who wish to resist the pressure to make choices they do not wish to make.

2028 and **2037** are **3** years, which are good times to grow a family, expand a business or career interest, and make a three-year plan; also, 3 years are good times for long-distance travel or relocation, lasting prosperity, justice, and gaining respect and authority.

2029 and **2038** are **4** years, when matters should stabilize. They are lucky for realizing property assets, renovations, and making modest (but steady) ongoing money, maybe resulting from earlier speculation or savings; 4 years can bring unexpected good fortune.

2030 and **2039** are **5** years and are good times for sudden job changes, travel (especially short trips), health improvement, success in speculation, short-term moves, and they are the friend of the renter. 5 years are lucky for learning new things and for passing tests or examinations. They are also good for communication, especially through the media.

2031 and **2040** are **6** years, which are lucky for romance, marriage, and emotional commitments, good fortune in every way, the mending of quarrels and estrangements, and gradual growth toward any goal.

2032 and **2041** are both **7** years, which are beneficial for all types of fertility and all matters connected to mothers, women, and passing from one stage of womanhood to another. Years that correspond with 7 are good for spiritual awareness and the revealing of secrets, as well as finding new love after loss or betrayal.

2033 and **2042** are **8** years, which are lucky for gaining power, achievement (especially in literary or creative matters), gaining status and recognition in career, major business success leading to long-term wealth, and transformation of life in the way most desired.

2034 and **2043** are **9** years, bringing luck as well as the determination to overcome all challenges and conflicts. Years that correspond with 9 are the best for coming out on top, achieving success in whatever has or is being sought, and actions or activities, especially sports, that open new doors to acclaim.

Then the cycle begins again: **2044** is a **1** year, **2045** a **2** year, **2046** a **3** year, and so on.

Calculating the Best Times

This part is remarkably simple: Decide which number is luckiest in a particular situation, checking the 1 to 9 meanings in the previous chapter. Again, 2 and 4, which relate to the master numbers 11 and 22, are especially fortunate. Knowing the strengths of each time can be useful for face-to-face communication, digital messages like texts and emails, and meetings held online, including those that will occur across time zones.

For example, if you want to initiate a new beginning, choose a 1 time as listed in the chart on pages 72–73 for a phone call or an email in which you plan to pitch a new idea, apply for a new job, or seek a loan for a solo business.

If you are in New York and want to talk to someone in the UK or Australia, you'll find that a 1 time is good for office hours in America or Australia. Scheduling a meeting or sending an email at this time is worth it, even if you need to get up early or stay up late because of the time zone difference.

Changing Your Luck

We all have a lucky number we may see repeatedly, perhaps in triplicate on a numbered license plate or as part of a phone number. It turns up when fate or circumstances seem to be overriding choice, and invariably all turns out well. You can change your own phone number to include it—the same goes for passwords. (Tip: A power number like 8 is good for protecting technology, so consider adding it to an especially important password.) In the final chapter, I will describe how to change bad luck into good fortune, even in terms of traditional unlucky dates like Friday the 13th that over many years have become tangled in superstition.

TWENTY-FOUR-HOUR CLOCK TIMES

and Corresponding Lucky Number Table

24-HR TIME	REG. TIME	LUCKY #
0000	12:00 a.m.	The time of no time—lucky for everything
0015	12:15 a.m.	6
0030	12:30 a.m.	3
0045	12:45 a.m.	9
0100	1:00 a.m.	1
0115	1:15 a.m.	7
0130	1:30 a.m.	4
0145	1:45 a.m.	1
0200	2:00 a.m.	2
0215	2:15 a.m.	8
0230	2:30 a.m.	5
0245	2:45 a.m.	2
0300	3:00 a.m.	3
0315	3:15 a.m.	9
0330	3:30 a.m.	6
0345	3:45 a.m.	3
0400	4:00 a.m.	4
0415	4:15 a.m.	1
0430	4:30 a.m.	7
0445	4:45 a.m.	4
0500	5:00 a.m.	5
0515	5:15 a.m.	2
0530	5:30 a.m.	8

24-HR TIME	REG. TIME	LUCKY #
0545	5:45 a.m.	5
0600	6:00 a.m.	6
0615	6:15 a.m.	3
0630	6:30 a.m.	9
0645	6:45 a.m.	6
0700	7:00 a.m.	7
0715	7:15 a.m.	4
0730	7:30 a.m.	1
0745	7:45 a.m.	7
0800	8:00 a.m.	8
0815	8:15 a.m.	5
0830	8:30 a.m.	2
0845	8:45 a.m.	8
0900	9:00 a.m.	9
0915	9:15 a.m.	6
0930	9:30 a.m.	3
0945	9:45 a.m.	9
1000	10:00 a.m.	1
1015	10:15 a.m.	7
1030	10:30 a.m.	4
1045	10:45 a.m.	1
1100	11:00 a.m.	2
1115	11:15 a.m.	8
1130	11:30 a.m.	5
1145	11:45 a.m.	2

24-HR TIME	REG. TIME	LUCKY #
1200	12:00 p.m.	3
1215	12:15 p.m.	9
1230	12:30 p.m.	6
1245	12:45 p.m.	3
1300	1:00 p.m.	4
1315	1:15 p.m.	1
1330	1:30 p.m.	7
1345	1:45 p.m.	4
1400	2:00 p.m.	5
1415	2:15 p.m.	2
1430	2:30 p.m.	8
1445	2:45 p.m.	5
1500	3:00 p.m.	6
1515	3:15 p.m.	3
1530	3:30 p.m.	9
1545	3:45 p.m.	6
1600	4:00 p.m.	7
1615	4:15 p.m.	4
1630	4:30 p.m.	1
1645	4:45 p.m.	7
1700	5:00 p.m.	8
1715	5:15 p.m.	5
1730	5:30 p.m.	2
1745	5:45 p.m.	8

24-HR TIME	REG. TIME	LUCKY #
1800	6:00 p.m.	9
1815	6:15 p.m.	6
1830	6:30 p.m.	3
1845	6:45 p.m.	9
1900	7:00 p.m.	1
1915	7:15 p.m.	7
1930	7:30 p.m.	4
1945	7:45 p.m.	1
2000	8:00 p.m.	2
2015	8:15 p.m.	8
2030	8:30 p.m.	5
2045	8:45 p.m.	2
2100	9:00 p.m.	3
2115	9:15 p.m.	9
2130	9:30 p.m.	6
2145	9:45 p.m.	3
2200	10:00 p.m.	4
2215	10:15 p.m.	1
2230	10:30 p.m.	7
2245	10:45 p.m.	4
2300	11:00 p.m.	5
2315	11:15 p.m.	2
2330	11:30 p.m.	8
2345	11:45 p.m.	5

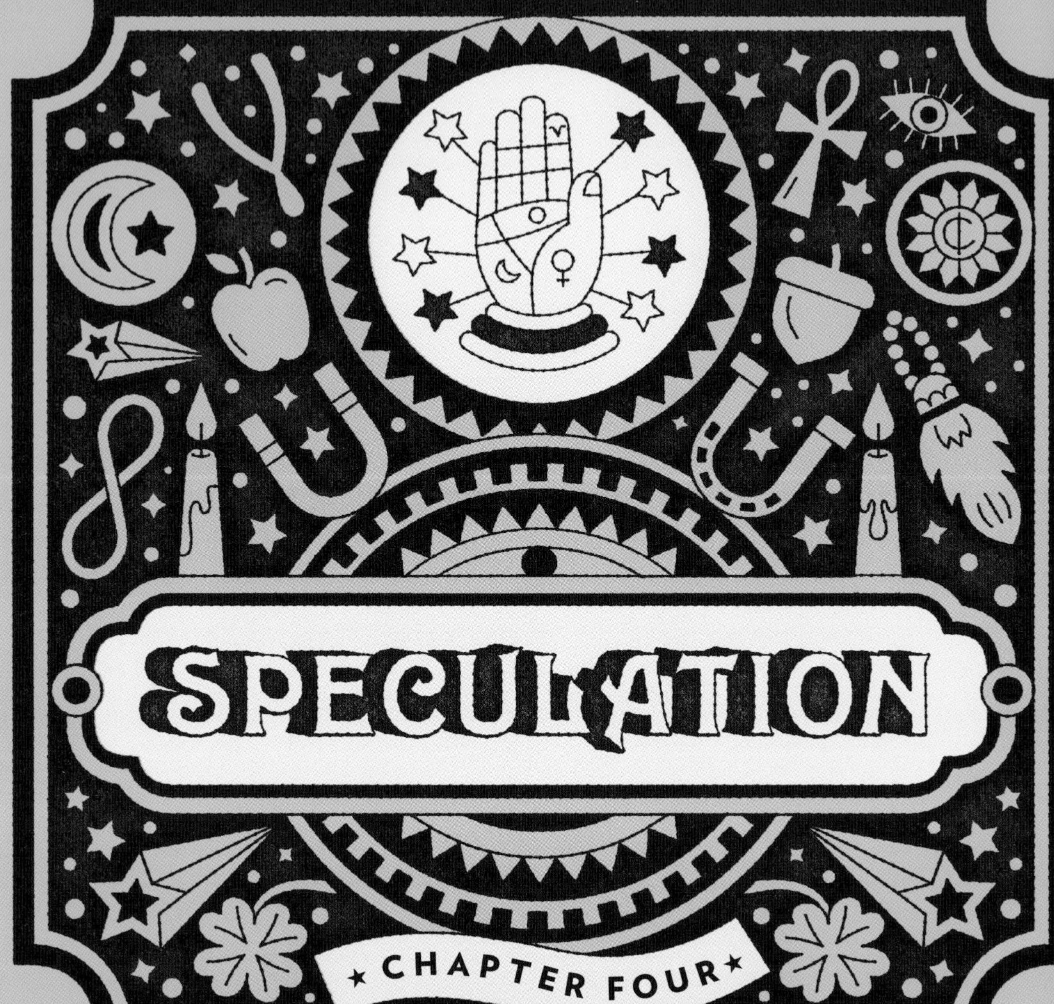
SPECULATION
CHAPTER FOUR

As far back as the sixth century BCE, the Greek philosopher Pythagoras believed that numbers were the key to the universe; harmonizing our lucky numbers at a particular time can tune into those universal energies. Whether you rely on your intuition, a talisman, or a lucky ritual to rake in big returns in games of chance, there are a few guidelines that could be helpful for you in this chapter.

This chapter does not promote reckless gambling or gambling addiction. Instead, by helping you develop intuition, it can actually discourage impulsive or compulsive gaming.

To Hold On to Your Luck While Gambling

Although many people develop their own gaming rituals and special charms to prevent luck from draining away while gambling, some methods have become popular worldwide. Here are several to consider:

- Rub a magnet five times over each side of a betting slip, lottery ticket, or a stock certificate before deciding whether to cash in the shares or buy more.
- If you have an itchy left (or nondominant hand) palm before gambling, money is coming; if the other palm is itchy, be more cautious, as money may drain out.
- Avoid offering or receiving fifty-dollar bills or a fifty-pound sterling note while gaming or buying chips.
- Don't count your gambling chips, especially when playing blackjack or poker, until you have finished playing.
- Don't whistle or hum at a gaming table.
- Before rolling them, blow three times on dice to imprint them with your personal luck energies.

- Wearing red underwear for luck is popular in China and other East Asian cultures, especially during the year of one's Chinese zodiac sign, which is believed to bring challenges and bad luck.
- If you were sitting or standing when you had your first big win, do that again in the future. But don't cross your legs, as that ties up fortune; cross your fingers instead.
- Don't look or walk away from the gaming table or slot machine after you have placed a bet.
- Tap gently on the side or screen of a slot machine or gaming computer to imprint the results with your good luck vibes.
- Along with your personal lucky numbers, as described in this chapter and Chapter 2, 7 is especially lucky in slot machines.
- An unlucky number for gambling is 13; 3 and 8 are lucky; 4 is regarded as inauspicious in China. If you repeatedly see a number before gambling, take it as a good omen for that number.
- Some groups believe you should hide lottery and raffle tickets to avoid them being jinxed. Place a blue anti-evil-eye crystal on them.
- Don't lend money to a friend at a casino, racecourse, or off-track betting site, as you will be giving away your luck.

- If luck is against a player in a card game, they can change it by getting up and walking around their chair three times.
- A pregnant woman holding gambling chips brings immense good luck. However, ask her to rub them on her belly (for ultimate luck) only if you know her very, very well.
- If possible, gain entry by a back or side door to a casino or building where a card game is being held, because by entering through the front door you may meet people leaving who have lost money.

Learning to Trust Your Instincts

The most successful professional brokers react immediately before the relevant information appears on the screen. Mumbo jumbo? Top tennis players anticipate and react to a tennis ball up to two seconds before it enters their line of sight.

Even seemingly random events are part of the ongoing energy field, like the eagle or leopard poised seconds before pouncing for prey. Gambling luck involves tuning into that instinctive *now* moment. The closest description of this intuitive *now* is the buzz of drinking too much coffee. The more you trust it in real-life situations, the more this primeval instinct kicks in to pick the winning lottery ticket.

Personal Lucky Numbers Based on Significant Dates

Earlier in this book you discovered your destiny number and applied it to finding the right home or the most auspicious date for a special occasion. These personal numbers can also offer predictive numbers for gaming if calculated from any approaching significant date, whether your birthday or that of a loved one, the birth of a child, or the anniversary of a wedding.

- Regard each separate number in this significant date as a lucky number. For gaming, use the current year (rather than the birth or anniversary year) with the day and month of the chosen event to link its numbers with the current energies. So if you were married on 2/4/1998 and the present year is 2026, you would use 2, 4, and 2026. Use the twenty-four-hour clock for times of birth, etc.
- If you have too many numbers, write the individual numbers on squares of paper and set them in a circle.
- Mix them, blank side up, holding your writing hand above the squares, and choose by *feel* the numbers you need.
- The strongest feeling will be over the luckiest numbers, so this method is best when only a single number is needed.

- You may find the single lucky number matches the reduced 1 through 9 or master 11 or 22 numerological equivalent of the name of a horse or company whose shares you are considering buying or selling against advice.

Tarot and Playing Cards for Choosing Lucky Numbers

If you have more time to make a choice, tarot cards and playing cards can give you information about the potential implications of your lucky numbers and if it is a good time to bet.

PLAYING CARDS

Pick a single card from a face-down shuffled pack of all four suits from Ace to 10, plus the Court cards for each and the two Jokers. The Jacks are valued at 3, the Queens 2, the Kings 1, and the Jokers 4. For example, if an Ace or King is drawn, you know that 1 is a lucky number. Now pick twice as many cards as you need lucky numbers, set them in pairs, and add the value of each of the pair to the other but do not reduce to a single digit.

Ignore the suit differences. For example, 3 of Spades plus 9 of Clubs gives you the lucky number 12. If the pair contains the same suit or number, is two Kings, etc., then the number is particularly lucky. If you get repeating numbers when adding your pairs, it means you have an especially lucky number.

If one pair has two 6s and you have 12 as a lucky number in another pair, take another pair from the shuffled face-down pack. Continue to take additional pairs from the deck if the repeated number recurs, but know it is extremely favorable.

If any numbers on the chosen cards predominate the pairs or are represented by Court cards of the same value, regardless of suit, those are especially lucky. If numbers recur regularly on different occasions, they may have special lucky significance for other games of chance, especially if you keep seeing, for example, double or triple 7s on number plates, house numbers, or in phone call numbers you receive.

If there is a majority of high numbers, winnings relating to those numbers may be swift but probably a single win rather than a series.

If there are more low numbers, luck may be slower off the ground or be more modest.

Three or more Kings is a good omen; if a Jack or Joker is present, be cautious of risking large amounts or betting your winnings.

A predominance of Diamonds in playing cards or Pentacles in the tarot (see pages 82–83 for more on the tarot) heralds a secure rather than spectacular financial gain; Hearts or Cups, a time to trust your intuition as to timing; Clubs or Wands are lucky risks connected with shares, travel prizes, games of skill including television quizzes, or business speculation. Spades suggest caution and being wary of a seeming quick fix.

Queen cards advise taking your time with stakes that may affect security, and quitting while ahead.

TAROT

Tarot is useful if you are choosing numbers of higher values, such as the Major Arcana cards, which number to 21 or 22 depending on the deck. The playing card rules (see pages 80–81 and above) apply here, too. Count Knights/Princes and Pages/Princesses as 3s and 4s, respectively.

The tarot Page or Princess warns against being too trusting of other players in card games, especially if a Magician appears. An illustrated pack such as the Rider-Waite or Morgan-Greer offers extra information. You don't need to know the fortune-telling meanings; simply look at the pictures as they tell the story.

The 8 of Wands, showing trees flying through the air and covered in growing leaves, promises luck where travel or a car or boat is a prize in a competition.

A predominance of Major Arcana cards (0 or 1 the Fool to 21 or 22 the World, depending on your tarot pack numbering) indicates that Lady Luck is on your side.

The Wheel of Fortune is best of all, especially if you are picking only one lucky number.

Court cards (representing people) suggest working together as a group (syndicate) can be beneficial.

Beware of sneaky or gloomy cards, often Swords. The 7 of Swords, which shows a man running away with the swords, could suggest that a particular gaming club or card school may be less than honest. The 10 of Swords, which portrays a figure with swords sticking out of their back, warns you to steer clear for now.

The Celestial cards—the Sun, Moon, and Star—are promising, but the Moon can be illusory, so don't bet the shirt on your back.

READING THE TAROT CARDS

Set out cards from a face-down shuffled pack for however many lucky numbers you need. If you wish, you can add them together to obtain an overall lucky number for any other form of gambling or speculation for which you need a single number (only reduce to a single digit if it feels right).

Lucky Charms for Games of Chance

This especially applies to gaming tables, lotteries, or card games. The ultimate traditional lucky charm—kept with personal cards used for gaming, on top of betting slips or lottery tickets, or taken to a casino—consists of three green crystals, traditionally green amazonite or aventurine or sometimes jade, in a green purse. You can choose repetitive words spoken aloud or in the mind before speculation, touching your charm bag to erase the doubting vibes. A common one is "Much haste, no time, the win is mine" or "As I chance my arm, keep calm to speculate and calculate the hand of fate." For competitions where chance plays a larger part than skill, a bag containing a green aventurine, an amazonite, and a black-and-white snowflake obsidian are substituted, all wrapped in a knotted green scarf.

The Ultimate Lucky Game of Chance Bag

This bag, which works well for every occasion of speculating or gambling, dates back to medieval times. By collecting charms, plants, and crystals relating to good fortune in a single bag, their energies combine and become imprinted with your own fortune-attracting energies through the "like attracts like" principle. Collect any of the following:

- A lucky hand root (the ultimate gambling plant, which is obtainable online but toxic) or a piece of dried grapevine
- A miniature 10 of Diamonds playing card
- Dried sage in a tiny bag
- A silver dollar or silver charm such as a four-leaf clover or horseshoe in silver or gold
- A token from an arcade or a gambling chip
- A green aventurine or amazonite crystal
- A white drawstring or leather bag or purse
- A white cord
- Traditionally a little whisky, sherry, port, or malt wine, or a couple of drops of rose essential oil

Make the bag on Wednesday, the day of Mercury, at sunset.

Place all the items in the bag or purse, adding a drop or two of alcohol or rose oil.

Tie the bag with three knots, saying three times, "Rich I'll be, for luck's with me."

Midsummer Eve is a traditional time to replace the bag, taking out the charms/dollar and burying the rest.

To Win Competitions or Raffles

Use a lucky horseshoe charm in gold or silver, with points tied upward with red ribbon to keep the good luck in, or a golden tiger eye and some dried cloves. On any Sunday, add the contents to a small gold bag, saying nine times fast as you close it, "Gold of fortune increased be, Lady Luck smile down on me."

For Fast Online Gaming

You will need uncooked popcorn in an airtight container. Before going online, cook the popcorn or heat it in a microwave, chanting "Pop, pop, pop, pop, and never stop; press the keys and win with ease and I will take the lot." Eat the popcorn while you are online gaming, chanting the rhyme fast in your mind if you get stuck.

For Online Bidding or Real-Time Auctions

If bidding through a website such as eBay, before going online, set three Chinese lucky coins or three gold- or copper-colored coins in front of your computer or tablet. Pick up and shake the coins three times while saying, "Make a bid, low not high, luck is rising to the skies, I outdo opposition and gain top position." Toss and catch them in open-cupped hands, set them in front of the device, and go online.

THE MOON
CHAPTER FIVE

You may recognize the phrase "when you wish upon a star" from the popular song, but in fact the moon is an even more effective target for hopes and dreams. For countless generations and throughout many lands, wishing on the moon has been considered a potent way to call in good fortune. And when both the moon and sun are shining in the sky at the same time, almost anything is possible.

Moon Luck

The moon changes shape throughout the month, and each shape, or phase, brings a special kind of luck. You can check the moon phases online or in books. After you have accessed these sources, you can instantly tap into the specific good fortune on offer throughout the month and year. Good fortune may be accessed when you first see the crescent moon; then, as the moon waxes, the momentum grows to offer even greater luck for your life. Finally comes the full moon—the most dynamic phase of all—whose luck-bringing vibes may be felt on the nights directly before and after the full moon (see https://www.timeanddate.com for the full moon rise time and date in your location). Mondays are lucky moon days even during the wane. A crescent, waxing, or full moon on a Monday is considered especially fortunate, and even more so if it occurs when the waxing or full moon passes through your zodiac sign. Silver is the lucky color and metal of the moon.

Lunar Wishes

Crescent, waxing, and full moon energies bring luck to the home and family matters, especially concerning the mother, children, and animals. The prime focus is fertility because the moon rules over all the ebbs and flows of the human body, mind, and psyche. The moon also encourages psychic development, clairvoyance, meaningful dreams, healing, successful gardening, keeping secrets, and reconciliation, with its fortune vibes building from crescent to full. Here are some tips for working with moon energies to maximize luck:

- Plant herbs of the moon three or four days before the appearance of the full moon, whether in the garden or in pots in the kitchen.
- Moon oils and herbs fill you with moon power if you bathe in them, burn them, or diffuse them. They can increase your own intuitive and psychic powers to discover opportunity, a major key to good luck. Herbs and oils of the moon include calamus, camphor, jasmine, lemon and lemon balm, moonwort, myrrh, and sandalwood.
- Carry crystals of the moon during the whole moon month, from full moon to full moon, re-empowering them on the full moon by leaving them in the moonlight from moon rise to set. Moon crystals and gems include moonstone, mother of pearl, satin spar, selenite, sea-green aquamarine, and pale golden beryl.
- Leave a tiny moonstone or silver charm in half an eggshell on the bedroom window ledge from the crescent to full moon to call in fertility if you hope to conceive a child and for fresh growth of all kinds into the home.

- Eat foods of the moon to absorb its power, from crescent to full, and to boost good fortune when the moon is on the wane. Foods of the moon include eggplants, coconuts, cucumbers, eggs, grapes, lettuce, melons, milk, and watercress.
- Wear silver jewelry, the moon's metal.
- Wear white, blue, or cream-colored clothes whenever you need to tune into your inner moon rhythms to allow positive energies to gently flow.
- St. Christopher silver medallions increase the natural protection and good fortune energies for travel, especially overseas and by night. Empowering your silver travel charms or a special silver pendant or bracelet on the full moon each month will keep you safe away from home, even during the wane.
- Place the flowers of the moon in your home, or plant them or silver bushes in your garden. Moon flowers include dahlia, gardenia, moonflower, jasmine, lotus, pink phlox, poppy, sweet William, wintergreen, and any small white flowers that are especially fragrant at night.
- Sit against a moon tree bathed in full moonlight. Moon trees include any growing close to water, but especially willow, mountain ash, mango tree, eucalyptus, rowan, and banana tree.

Blue Moon

A blue moon refers to either the second full moon in a calendar month or, traditionally, the third full moon in a season containing four full moons, which is very rare. The full blue moon, which is not visibly blue at all, is considered extra fortunate for the increase of fertility, all good fortune, and finances. For an urgent piece of luck, wish on the first blue moon of the month that your good fortune will come by the second blue moon.

Supermoon

This is when the full moon comes closest to the earth and so appears unusually bright and large. It can be seen clearly on the nights immediately before and after the full moon. The supermoon is ideal for longer-term or major endeavors and wishes, unlike an ordinary full moon, which is invoked to grant wishes by the next full moon.

The Moon and the Zodiac

Each month, the moon passes for approximately two and a half days through each zodiac sign, bringing good fortune to those born under that sign. Even more luck comes when the full moon rises in your birth sign, which happens approximately once a year, often around your half-birthday, giving you an extra chance to connect with unique fortune-attracting vibes. However, you can borrow the strengths of any zodiac birth sign when the full moon travels through it.

The thirteen full moons each year were once linked with Neolithic and even Paleolithic goddess worship, and that is a reason why the number 13 became regarded as unlucky in the eyes of patriarchal religion. To maximize each of the full moons, use the suggested herbs (in cooking, as teas, as essential oils, planted in the garden, or as potted herbs) as well as the suggested crystals associated with each zodiac sign. You can also burn candles in the colors of the zodiac sign from when the full moon enters until the moon leaves the sign. I have suggested herbs that are available all year. The phases of the moon, especially from crescent to full, are generally considered the most fortunate times for zodiac connections. However, even during the waning moon, when the moon is getting smaller, you can still have good luck if the moon happens to align with your birth zodiac sign, bringing extra lunar and zodiac energy.

MOON IN ARIES

Brings luck in matters of courage, independence, self-reliance, self-employment, action, sports and activities, health, launching major life changes, energy and passion, and overcoming intimidation

Crystal: red jasper
Color: red
Herbs: basil, cinnamon, ginger, parsley

MOON IN TAURUS

Brings luck in fertility, love, increasing radiance, money, material security, acquiring beautiful things, and driving away debt

Crystal: rose quartz
Color: pink
Herbs: sorrel, rose petals, vervain

MOON IN GEMINI

For luck in speculation and games of chance, passing examinations and tests, healing energies, communication (especially media), short-term travel and moves; a particularly lucky moon time to reverse bad luck

Crystal: citrine
Color: yellow
Herbs: fennel, lavender, lemongrass, rosemary

MOON IN CANCER

For happiness and protection of home and family; conception, mothers, children, and fidelity; keeping secrets; the ultimate moon sign

Crystal: moonstone
Color: silver
Herbs: aloe vera, clary sage, lemon verbena

MOON IN LEO

For success, power, leadership, fame, prosperity, career and abundance, potency, and childbirth; a good time for applying for jobs and shining in the workplace

Crystal: amber
Color: gold
Herbs: angelica, chamomile, rosemary

MOON IN VIRGO

For all health and healing, animals, any detailed matters, employment, skill with arts and crafts, gardening, adhering to diets and fitness regimes

Crystals: peridot, olivine
Color: green
Herbs: marjoram, mint, patchouli

MOON IN LIBRA

For romance, marriage, and partnerships; peace and harmony; justice and the successful outcome of court cases; charisma and compromise

Crystal: blue lace agate
Color: blue
Herbs: bergamot, thyme, vanilla

MOON IN SCORPIO

For transformation, retraining, and relocating; passionate sex, increased psychic powers, and any strongly felt desires or needs; recovering what has been lost or stolen; removes bad luck

Crystals: opal, obsidian
Colors: indigo, burgundy
Herbs: catnip, coriander, pennyroyal

MOON IN SAGITTARIUS

For travel, adventures, long-distance moves, horses, creative ventures, happiness and optimism, good ideas, sports, reversing money losses, and finding lost pets

Crystal: turquoise
Color: orange
Herbs: cloves, hyssop, sage

MOON IN CAPRICORN

For commitment in love and business, financial security, all official matters, wise caution, older people, steady promotion and stable business ventures, overcoming obstacles though persistent effort, animals, releasing money that is tied up or disputed

Crystal: garnet
Colors: dark red, brown
Herbs: caraway, mugwort, tarragon, vetivert, patchouli

MOON IN AQUARIUS

For moving life forward in unique ways, success of inventions and moneymaking plans, friendships, alternative therapies

Crystal: amethyst
Color: purple
Herbs: benzoin, nutmeg, valerian

MOON IN PISCES

For new love or love after loss, music and the performing arts, balancing two commitments or two careers, adaptability, merging two families, telepathic powers, overcoming people or demands pulling you in different directions

Crystals: bloodstone/heliotrope, clear quartz
Color: white
Herbs: borage, lemon, sweetgrass

LUCKY MOON ACTIVITIES

crescent moon luck

When you first see the crescent moon in the sky, turn over three silver coins in your open-cupped hands facing the moon and say three times these age-old words: "New moon, true moon, moon in the stream, bring the good fortune of which I dream." It is said that by the full moon your finances will have improved. Adapt the words of the rhyme for any need, and they are luckiest spoken near water. For love or commitment, place a silver ring on your wedding finger or a silver heart pendant around your neck, and for travel wear a St. Christopher medallion.

waxing moon luck

The waxing or increasing phase is especially fortunate on the three nights before the full moon. A waxing moon is lucky for making a new beginning or starting a new venture; working toward a longer-term goal; improving health; gradually increasing prosperity; attracting good luck; enhancing fertility; finding friendship, new love, and romance; hunting for a job; and making plans for the future. Book an active, fun vacation to be taken during this period. Get up early every morning and use the extra time to give your day a flying start.

full moon luck

Traditionally the full moon is potent for love and major issues requiring an extra dose of good fortune. Full moon energies are especially lucky for fulfilling an immediate need, boosting power or courage, protecting yourself psychically or emotionally from malice, raising a large sum of urgently needed money, consummating love or conceiving a child, making a permanent love commitment, and make-or-break talks in a shaky relationship.

Because the time around the full moon can cause restlessness, try to channel your natural desire for change and action in order to avoid irritability or change for change's sake. Do something decisive and positive. Send off your novel, propose to your beloved, or ask your boss for a raise or a promotion. If you want to move, put your house on the market right before the full moon. The waning moon in the days following can reduce the attachment we feel to our home.

luck during the waning period

Although the waning moon will not attract good luck in itself, you can wear or carry extra silver charms or jewelry, or cook moon foods to maintain existing lunar good fortune. You can also use this period when the moon shrinks until it is no longer visible to remove misfortune. You can use the wane for banishing guilt or sorrow, or peacefully ending a relationship that has run its course, by reducing the crescent's hold on addictions and compulsions. Use the waning moon toward the end of the first week after the full moon to help quit smoking or overcome minor phobias. If you have debt problems, use the waning moon period when the moon appears late and is slender to get financial advice so that by the time the waxing moon comes you will be ready with a strategy.

MILESTONES
CHAPTER SIX

Milestones—whether annual seasonal holidays or once-in-a-lifetime events such as a wedding or birth—are important focuses for increasing good fortune. Many ancient customs accompanying these celebrations are still practiced, although their origins may be lost. It was believed that these customs kept evil spirits at bay during a time when life was more hazardous. Today, you can tap into the positive vibes of symbolic actions and words accumulated through the ages when good fortune, albeit of a different kind, is needed.

Lucky Festivals

Below are some important celebrations that have accumulated a number of customs either to bring luck in or to banish negative energies.

HALLOWEEN

Halloween and the two days following it are traditionally the time for recalling ancestors and asking for their help for the year ahead (it was once the beginning of the Celtic New Year). Their blessings can be invoked by displaying the favorite flowers of these departed relatives, cooking their signature recipes, and perusing old family photos, recounting memories and eccentricities. According to the Scottish poet Robert Burns, Halloween is also a love festival: a celebration not of fear, but of fun and earthly pleasures.

Here is a Halloween custom meant to bring in good luck: To summon your dream lover, whether a known person or one not yet met, just before midnight light a candle placed so that it shines in a mirror. Face the mirror and eat an apple, which is an old love and fertility symbol. When you have eaten half, brush your hair with one hundred strokes while continuing to gaze in the mirror. Blow out the candle, and in the afterglow you may see your true love's image in the mirror next to you. If no image emerges, close your eyes and a picture of that person will come into your mind. If you are not yet committed, this may be someone you know but had considered only as a friend. Eat the rest of the apple, go to sleep, and according to the old beliefs you will dream of your love.

In Old Scots, a language spoken in Scotland from the fourteenth to seventeenth centuries, and in northern England, Halloween is also known as Nut-Crack Night. From Celtic times, nuts were a sacred Druidic food because the hazel was considered a magical tree. To discover whom you will marry, name each nut you put in the fire (which could be a bonfire or barbecue) after a desired or potential partner. The nut that cracks first will be your true love. You can adapt this hazelnut ritual for other issues involving choice, such as career or travel. You can also play with five people by placing five nuts on the fire, one for each player. The first nut to crack will be that of the first person to marry or have a baby (or grandchild), the second nut to crack foretells a long journey for its owner, the third will come into money, the fourth will find love from overseas or another state, and the fifth will have many secrets.

Two more Halloween-related traditions are: If you go to a crossroads at midnight on Halloween and listen to the wind, you will hear all you need to know for the coming twelve months; and children born on Halloween will be protected throughout life and enjoy second sight.

THANKSGIVING

Abraham Lincoln officially established Thanksgiving Day in America in 1863. Every year the US president ceremonially spares two Thanksgiving turkeys at the White House, which are sent to a farm to enjoy their liberty. Here are a few Thanksgiving rituals for good luck: On

Thanksgiving Eve, hang a whole orange in the room where you will hold the feast to bring or restore good fortune. First stick cloves all over the fruit, making wishes for yourself and others who will be present. Let the cloves pierce the skin, not the fruit. Roll the orange in powdered spice on a plate and tie it with red ribbon.

You may also create a Thankful, Thanksgiving, or Gratitude tree, not only to express gratitude for blessings received in the previous year, but also to attract advantages in the year ahead. Write your blessings, both for your home and workplace, on paper and attach them to a tree. If you are not using a live tree, you could take willow branches or tall fall foliage and decorate with acorns and leaves.

At the Thanksgiving feast, let each person touch the center of their piece of pecan or pumpkin pie before eating and give thanks for the year, even if it was not ideal, along with naming blessings desired for the coming twelve months.

Hide dried pine needles and nuts with a small gold item in an orange bag or knotted cloth within the branches of a Yule or Thanksgiving tree to attract prosperity and good fortune through the winter and to give thanks for what has been received.

CHRISTMAS/YULE

To counteract the commercialism of Christmas, old customs have survived that generate the abundance, love, and joy that are in the true spirit of

Christmas. Not only do they have the benefit of accumulated power created by generations of practice, but they also originate in the energy of love, which is inherently lucky. Here are a few to sample:

Light or make your own bayberry candles on Christmas Eve and New Year's Eve or anoint a green candle with bayberry oil before lighting. Lovers parted at Yule will be reunited through the delicate fragrance wherever they burn their bayberry candle.

You can also make Christmas Eve bayberry luck bags. Add nine dried bayberries to a charm bag with parsley, sage, rosemary, and thyme, which is lucky for successful business ventures and making accurate predictions in speculation or investments.

Sprinkle powdered bayberry root into a jar of coins until it is full. Seal the jar and shake it every morning of the week before Christmas to draw money, family happiness, and career opportunities to you.

Dumb cakes, made of oats, barley, and water, are made in silence and placed in the oven late in the evening by those seeking to see their future love on Christmas Eve. At midnight, according to old custom, the kitchen door will open and your true love will come in astral form and turn the cakes. More realistically you will dream of your future love and meet them before you make the dumb cakes again next year.

Make your own Christmas pudding or cake on Stir-up Sunday (the Sunday before Advent), or an earlier Sunday to allow it to mature, when family and friends and even the youngest child take turns stirring the pudding clockwise and making a silent wish. The Christmas pudding, originally a semiliquid concoction, contained the fruits and grains of the earth and, because of the coins and charms placed in it, the metals of the earth, thus ensuring prosperity, health, and happiness, especially for the person finding the charm (taking care if children are present). This promises family unity if the family members make and stir the pudding or cake together.

On the evening of the shortest day, around December 21, or on Christmas Eve before sunset, an occasion celebrated from time immemorial to anticipate the return of light and longer days, light a purple candle and in it burn dried sage to represent any misfortune that has befallen you or family or friends or that you fear may still happen.

On the days before Christmas, call in good fortune early. Stop the frantic shopping; decorate the home with sprigs of holly, ivy, and mistletoe; put up your Christmas tree; and make paper chains or homemade decorations as you did when you were a child.

NEW YEAR'S EVE

New Year's Eve is a wonderful time to celebrate the passing of the old year and the beginning of the new, and of course is associated with creating resolutions. However, there are a few other luck-bringing rituals you should consider alongside the familiar traditions. For example, on New Year's Eve, take a single-sheet calendar of the current year with squares for each day until

December 31. Cross out any days you would be happy to forget. Say, "Old year burn, bad luck, do not return" as you tear off a corner of the calendar, then burn that corner. Rip the rest to shreds a few minutes before midnight and throw it in the trash outdoors. Replace it after midnight with a new calendar beginning with January 1, marking the first square with a huge tick and saying, "New year, new fortune, enter here, bring a year only of good luck and cheer."

The traditional Scottish way to bring New Year good luck and prosperity into your home is a First Footing ceremony dating who knows how far back. Take a small bag, and place the following items in it before midnight: for sufficient money throughout the year—add copper, silver, or a gold-colored coin or item; for a healthy, happy, united home and companionship—add wrapped candies, dried fruits, nuts, dried basil, juniper berries, sage, or thyme; for enough practical resources for the year ahead—add a piece of coal or wood.

Five minutes before midnight, send a dark-haired person (or someone wearing a dark-colored hood) outside the front door with the bag as the First Footer to enter and bring good fortune. At midnight all shout, "Come in, New Year, New Year, you are welcome," while rattling pans and making other noise. The First Footer enters, shuts the door, and goes out the back door (if there is one) or out the front door, saying, "Out you go, Old Year, Old luck, Your time is past." The First Footer enters again, slams the door, walks upstairs to the top of the house and down again, shouting "Happy New Year!"

The First Footer deposits the bag on the hearth or in front of a burning white candle. All toast the New Year while making New Year wishes and resolutions.

Sweep bad luck out the front door before midnight and throw away the old broom. Do not throw out any of the party garbage, sweep, vacuum, or wash clothes until January 2, or you will also put out the New Year luck you have welcomed in.

Do not lend anything, especially money, on New Year's Day, or else you will be lending all year.

Lucky Milestones

You need not wait until a festival to use an occasion to bring in luck. Read on for suggestions to accompany happy events like births and weddings.

FOR A NEW BABY

From Scotland to West Africa and India, there are variations on a common belief that if knots in a cord are untied and locks opened while a woman is in labor, the birth will be easier. The psychological principle is that as those emotionally connected with the woman giving birth release their energies, they will aid the woman through these symbolic actions. Locks on doors or drawers are opened with a key. If the birth is slow, bottles will be uncorked and the liquid poured under running water, and windows and doors thrown open.

A newborn baby should traditionally be carried upstairs when brought home for the first time (if there is no second floor, then holding the baby while standing on a chair or high doorstep serves just as well) so that the child will become powerful in the world and gain riches and recognition.

Pregnant or nursing mothers are, in parts of Eastern Europe, encouraged to be present at the planting of the crops. In parts of Bavaria and Austria, a cherry tree is said to always be rich with fruit if a woman who has just given birth to her first child eats the first fruits.

In Celtic days in the crossover between Celtic paganism, which included Druidism, and Christianity, where infant mortality was high, a baptism was performed immediately after the child was born, and involved the mother, the midwife, a special nurse called *ban-ghluin*, plus the father. The Celtic midwife placed three drops of water on the newborn infant's head. The child was thus anointed with the power and protection of sky, sea, and land. The nurse would then administer the *baisteadh breith* or birth baptism, bathing the child for the first time in water in which a gold and silver coin were placed as symbolic of the powers of the sun and moon. Holding the child over the bath, the nurse would fill her palm with water nine times and rub it over the child while singing a blessing incantation. Each handful of water would endow an attribute on the child, rather like the concept of the good fairies in "Sleeping Beauty." These gifts included gentle speech, generosity of spirit, wealth, health, and grace.

In the United Kingdom, babies born while bells chime, especially on the New Year, are believed to possess healing powers and be especially psychic.

FOR A NEW HOME

When moving to a new house, paint the porch blue (or, if in a shared house or apartment, a wall in your room) and sprinkle salt on the doorstep or your personal entrance to attract good fortune and keep bad luck and malevolent influences away.

Scatter coins as you enter the property for the first time as your own to bring prosperity.

Never take a broom with you when moving house. Buy a new one to keep outside the front door, bristles up, or a small hearth brush in a shared apartment or house. Sweep the old energies out the front door.

FOR A WEDDING OR RENEWAL OF VOWS

Although rain on the wedding day is considered lucky, if the sun breaks through as the couple leaves the marriage place, there will be great luck in their future.

In many cultures, the centerpiece of the wedding feast or breakfast is the wedding cake. The rich contents of the dessert indicate the good things of life: the fruits, grains, and spices of the earth. The bride or couple cuts the cake to ensure their fertility in the way most desired. Everyone present must eat a piece to strengthen the good fortune, and pieces are sent to absent friends for the same reason.

An unmarried woman should pass a crumb of her piece of cake through a wedding or gold ring three times before putting the crumb under their pillow to dream of future love.

A couple keeps a piece of the cake to ensure they remain faithful, and a tier is often preserved for the christening of the first child, first anniversary, or another major milestone in the relationship.

Crying at a wedding promises there will be no more tears, but pearls are not considered lucky as a gift, as they resemble teardrops.

When the wedding bouquet is tossed over the bride's shoulder at the reception, whoever catches it will be next to have a permanent commitment or, if already married, will know great happiness.

The best days to get married are, according to an old rhyme, Monday for health, Tuesday for wealth, and Wednesday, the best day of all.

Tradition recommends that the bride wears something old—perhaps a family treasure as a symbol of her heritage and her ancestors—something new to mark the beginning of the new life, something borrowed from a happy person who is married or in a stable relationship, and something blue such as a ribbon or flower for fidelity. A silver coin in the left shoe of one or both of the couple brings prosperity.

BAD LUCK
CHAPTER SEVEN

Sometimes it's not enough to generate good luck; you may feel like you are cursed, or that an evil energy is following you. Perhaps you've had a string of setbacks that has developed into anxiety that you just can't shake (see pages 10–11). Whatever the reason, addressing the negativity can be useful before attempting to bring in positive vibes. All the remedies in this chapter can counter bad luck and shield against misfortune. At the same time, they are lucky symbols in their own right.

Resisting Misfortune

First, you don't have to accept bad luck, curses, jinxes, or the ill wishes of those who tell you they have employed a magical practitioner to hex you or who simply speak or act maliciously toward you. Usually they have watched one too many horror movies. Nevertheless, this can be unsettling, despite the rational part of us arguing that it is not possible.

Returning Misfortune

Invariably, gossips are driven to tell you when someone has sent bad luck your way or made a derogatory remark about you. When they do, subtly push your hands away from your body, palms upright and fingers together, and toward them as they are talking. Think, *You can have that back.* This works because we are putting up energy barriers against attacks on confidence and luck. Like a ball bouncing against a wall, those negative energies forcefully return to the sender and bearer of doom.

Jinxing

This phenomenon can be even more unconsciously disturbing than gossip, and even logical people may fear they have jinxed themselves and sabotaged their efforts if they either speak overconfidently about a plan or, more commonly, talk about failing. We may recall those family superstitions fed to us in childhood like "Don't count your chickens before they are hatched," "Pride goes before a fall," etc. There is a widespread belief that we can trip ourselves up through anxiety before we even try to accomplish what we desire. There is also a belief that jinxes can begin to stick to other concerns and then become hard to shake off.

However, there are lots of ways to get rid of a jinx, whether it is imposed by jealous people or our own insecurities. These remedies work equally well if someone has spooked you with a curse or a denigration. A quick reversal clears the decks, both psychologically and energy-wise, by countering words and actions, rejecting the concept that anyone can bring misfortune to us by ill-wishing or that fate must be unchangeable. How we react, whether to a fear of jinxing or an unavoidable mishap, is the difference between recovering quickly or accepting victimhood.

To reverse a jinx, try one of the following solutions: Write the jinx on paper in soluble ink and dissolve it in water. Using chalk, etch it on a chalkboard or paving stone and pour water over it or wait for rain. Cross and uncross your fingers behind your back nine times while increasing the speed of the motion and repeating faster and faster in your mind, *Jinx, Jinx, Jinx, with your trouble and strife, be gone from my life*. If that doesn't work, tap on a table three times loudly after jinxing yourself, or subtly if someone present denigrates you.

If thoughts of failure or bad luck fill your mind or disturb your sleep, chant in your head or aloud, *Lucky, lucky, luckier shall I be, Bad luck no more shall follow me*. If bad things seem to happen after a certain important family relative visits or after a confrontation, if minor sicknesses linger, or if worries about debt sour the atmosphere, burn or diffuse fragrance oils with protective and luck-bringing properties in your home before the visit or after a quarrel, when plagued by illness, or while experiencing financial difficulties.

Alternatively, add oils to a bucket of warm water and mop or scrub negativity away. The best such oils are cedarwood, eucalyptus, geranium, lavender, lemon, myrrh, neroli, orange, peppermint, pine, rose, and sandalwood. Lemon is also an instant energizer and can focus thoughts. Peppermint, cedarwood, and sandalwood offer protection against gossip or hostility and stimulate positive counterresponses in you. Use orange and lavender mixes for stimulating friendly communication at home or work and for resolving personal problems or intercolleague friction in the workplace that is affecting the general atmosphere. At work, add a couple of drops of oil to a cup of warm water and place on your desk or work bench, add it to cotton wool on a saucer in a warm place, or wear an aroma bracelet with beads infused with the diluted oil.

Glyphs to Filter out Misfortune

From ancient times, hieroglyphs guided the Egyptians safely through the perils of the afterlife. Certain glyphs from various cultures, when worn, etched, or painted on wood or crystals, have acted as shields from negative energies. Their power continues to this day. Some of the glyphs, especially Egyptian ones or the *Om* or infinity symbols, are popularly sold as jewelry and especially as pendants, to be touched whenever anxiety intrudes or matters take a bad turn.

ANCIENT EGYPTIAN HIEROGLYPHS

Ankh

This symbol carries a double meaning: First, of eternal life, as it guards against ill health and replaces it with energy, charisma, radiance, and well-being. The ankh is protective against ageism in the workplace. This symbol also signifies unity because of its associations with the love between the goddess Isis and her consort Osiris. This makes the ankh very defensive in a relationship if you experience opposition or have concerns about fidelity. It can also help attract and maintain twin soul love. The ankh is often in the form of a silver charm.

Scarab

The scarab beetle represents the scarab-headed Khepri, god of the sun at dawn who rolled the sun wheel before him, bringing each new day. This amulet was a profound symbol of rebirth to the Egyptians and shields against loss as well as those who try to destroy happiness or security. It heralds new beginnings at times when you are experiencing stagnation. In the modern world, it signifies fierce protection against all danger, verbal attack, and injustice, while also opening the potential of each new day for you.

Eye of Horus

Linked with the all-seeing moon eye of the sky god Horus or sometimes the sun god Ra, this symbol is a powerful defensive hieroglyph, especially when worn as a silver or gold charm, or one made of lapis lazuli, blue faience, or any blue stone. Alternatively, you can trace an eye shape every morning with the index finger of your writing hand over a blue crystal pendant or charm to create a barrier against harm. Protective against what used to be called the evil eye, in the modern world the Eye of Horus repels envy, jealousy, spite, and gossip.

SYMBOLS FROM OTHER CULTURES

Perfect Action

A lesser-known symbol also referred to as a wish, or good luck, symbol, this character can be drawn in the air in front of you every morning, whether in the home or workplace, to break a run of bad luck. Start with the left hand and trace a counterclockwise spiral, followed by a clockwise spiral using the right hand. You can find pendants depicting this symbol online, whether made of silver or gold or outlined in green stones. The Perfect Action symbol is deeply protective and will preserve the best in family, love, and home. If matters regarding another person, animal, or situation are uncertain in terms of outcome, look to this glyph.

Infinity

The infinity symbol, also called the Gateway to Eternity, is much more popular than the Perfect Action symbol and very easily obtainable as a charm or a pendant. Infinity is easy to draw if you are making your own charm; start in the center and make the loop on the right side of the symbol, and cross back over the center to make the left-hand loop. An infinity symbol is the ultimate glyph for health, healing, and long life, and it is deeply protective. Infinity sends positive energies to children, even over a distance, when they are far away from home. This is also a good symbol to protect a teenager who has undesirable friends. Try embroidering the symbol in the lining of their favorite garment for inobtrusive protection. Infinity symbols also improve general health in situations where stress or worry is making a condition worse.

Aum, Ohm, or Om

In Sanskrit, *Aum*, *Ohm*, or *Om* is the first primal or sacred sound that brought the whole universe into being. It represents creation working together as a single unit.

Either spoken as a continuous chant or worn as a pendant in gold or silver, Om is a symbol of integration and unity, bringing life into harmony if out of balance. It is excellent for calming any stress as well as workaholic or hyperactive tendencies. In peace rituals, whether for families, the community, or globally, it has an impressive reach. It can also be healing for insomnia or an inability to relax. Because each act of creation is regarded in ancient cultures as a repetition of the first creation of the universe, it is resonant and long-lasting.

VIKING RUNES

Fehu

Increasingly, runes are burned on disks of wood as pendants, charms, or part of a rune set. Alternatively, you may find them painted in red on a branch or stake of wood and planted in the garden facing outward to defend the home against harm and to attract good fortune. The rune Fehu is the ultimate symbol of wealth through hard work, as well as financial stability through overcoming debt or financial hazards in uncertain times. It is also deeply protective in situations where others ask too much of us or we are expected to make sacrifices that have too high an emotional price.

Perthro

Perthro is associated with the rune cup, a game of chance in which the ancient warriors tested their luck. Because of this, it has become a symbol of bad luck turning into good. Etched on a disk of wood and kept in a red bag as a charm or made into a pendant, Perthro is effective if identity or beliefs are under threat, or if you must work where you disagree with the ethics of the business. It is also protective against those who try to control you by mind manipulation or guilt.

Counteracting Specific Bad Luck Experiences

It is possible to avoid certain experiences associated with bad luck, but if they unfortunately do happen, you may wish to protect against a recurrence. Read on for ways to do both.

ACCIDENTS

Guaranteed to spook the most logic-rooted souls, the old saying that accidents or troubles come in threes may be imprinted on our subconscious from childhood. Two accidents, even if unrelated, have us waiting for the third, which can be attracted by jitteriness or anxiety.

Dating to fourteenth-century Europe is the belief that this "rule of three" can be counteracted by deliberately smashing a cracked plate; a more recent belief is that deliberately dropping a dollar bill where it will be found once you have moved on will turn *your* loss into someone else's gain.

A BROKEN MIRROR

It's hard to remain immune to the superstition dating from ancient Greek times that a mirror reflection held your soul, and if the mirror was broken the soul would take seven years to regrow. Until recently, mirrors were covered when someone died to prevent the soul from becoming trapped.

However, in other traditions including feng shui, a mirror is placed facing the front door to reflect back bad fortune and magnify the good that is entering. In the event of a broken mirror:

- Carefully wrap the broken mirror pieces in a piece of strong fabric while saying, "Seven years of misfortune now are bound, seven years of good luck will be found."
- Throw away or bury safely the mirror shards in the cloth and buy a replacement mirror. Set seven flowers in front of it, saying, "Seven times seven, good fortune's mine. This mirror with best luck always shall shine."

DOMESTIC ILL FORTUNE

To access the ultimate protective domestic substance, you need only to reach for what is perhaps the most common seasoning: simple table salt. Keep a dish of salt in the kitchen to absorb the day's negativity. Leave another near the front door to deflect any challenges of the day from returning. Replace both dishes at bedtime and wash the salt away. Some people hide twists of salt in a workplace drawer, glove compartment of a car, or their bag or briefcase, replacing them on the last day of each month.

Sweep salt outward from a doorstep to brush away misfortune. Salt scattered on stages to keep misfortune away from theatrical performances is still practiced in countries such as Japan. Salt is also believed to symbolize domestic happiness. In olden times, the ancestral salt box was handed down from generation to generation as a way of preserving family unity. A family heirloom salt cellar carries the protection and love of family past.

Make sure you never run out of salt because, as it is said, "Short of salt, short of money." Do not hand the salt cellar to a person who asks at the table; rather, set it near them to avoid giving away your luck. Salt is often thrown over the left shoulder if it is spilled, following an ancient belief of throwing it in the eye of the devil. In modern times, spilling salt is held as a sign that money will flow out if salt is not then cast over the left shoulder.

There is another common kitchen ingredient that is similarly effective for dispelling bad luck energies in the home: garlic. Reach for a bulb when you want to protect your family. The old belief is that garlic repels vampires. Nonetheless, a garlic-flavored meal can be helpful at any time to repel those who leech off you emotionally or financially. If you're dining with such a person, surreptitiously serve yourself a portion of the meal without garlic.

A string of garlic on the kitchen ceiling traditionally keeps away all danger from the home and guards against accidents in the kitchen. Replace the string when the cloves begin to shrivel, but do not eat the garlic.

CONCLUSION

Supercharge Your Luck

Within these pages, I have recalled traditional and modern ways in which good luck can be attracted and misfortune avoided or reversed.

Even if you do not have a superstitious bone in your body, sometimes Lady Luck can knock us off course or others' negativity can lead us to doubt ourselves. This may close us off to good fortune that may be available when we are aware and receptive to people who appear at the right time in the right place, or opportunities that may help us make or remake our fortune. As well as "thinking lucky," if we act and speak using methods filled with power practiced over centuries, we can turn around our mindset and become lucky again.

May good fortune follow you for all your days.

ACKNOWLEDGMENTS

To my beloved children, Tom, Jade, Jack, Miranda, and Bill, and my beautiful grandchildren, Freya, Holly, Oliver, and Sophie. To John Gold, my copy editor, protector, and mentor; and Kornelia Gold, my inspiration and wonderful friend. Finally, my sincere gratitude to the team at Union Square & Co.: Kate Zimmermann, former executive editor; Barbara Berger, executive editor; Kristin Mandaglio, project editor; Sandy Noman, production manager; Stacy Wakefield Forte, interior designer; and Nolan Pelletier, cover designer and interior artist.

ABOUT THE AUTHOR

CASSANDRA EASON is one of the most prolific and popular authors of our time, writing on all aspects of spirituality and magic, in addition to lecturing, broadcasting, and facilitating workshops throughout the world.

Cassandra has over 130 titles to her name, many of which have been translated into numerous languages, including Japanese, Russian, Hebrew, Portuguese, German, Dutch, and Spanish, which have established her as a worldwide best-selling author. Among her bestsellers are *A Spell a Day*, *A Little Bit of Palmistry*, and the 1001 series (*1001 Spells*, *1001 Dreams*, *1001 Tarot Spreads*, *1001 Crystals*, and *1001 Magical Plants*).

Her books have been serialized around the world, including in the *Daily Mail*, the *Daily Mirror*, *People* magazine, and *The Sun*, as well as in *Spirit and Destiny*, *Fate and Fortune*, *Prediction*, *Homes & Gardens*, *Good Housekeeping*, and in *Woman's Day* and *New Idea* in Australia. She had her own psychic column in the women's magazine *Best* and in *Writers' News*, and produced a monthly psychic master class for *Beyond* magazine..

In The United Kingdom, Cassandra had her own weekly miniseries, *Sixth Sense*, on United Artists cable network for a number of years before moving on to the Granada Breeze channel, where she was resident white witch for over two years on *Psychic Live Time*. She acted as psychic consultant/resident expert on the successful ITV series *Magic and Mystery* and has also analyzed dreams on the UK's Channel 4 *Big Brother* (seasons 3 and 4), as well as *Celebrity Big Brother*.

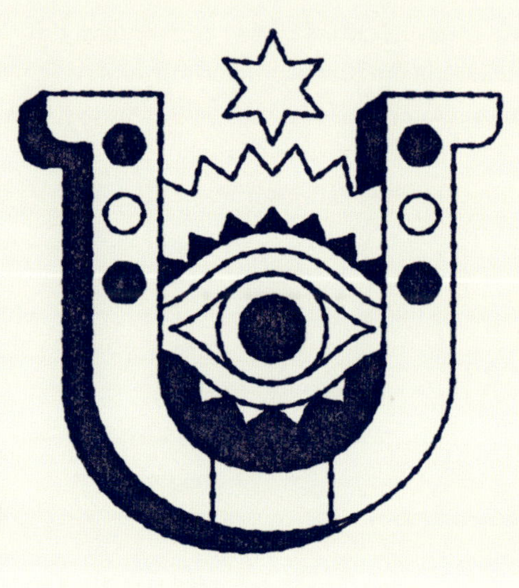